1/2/2011

It'll Come
In Useful
One Day

To Angela

Good luck with
the pear tree

RogerBryan

It'll Come In Useful One Day

Intriguing Ways to Jog Your Memory

ROGER BRYAN

Illustrators: Michael Heath, Ron McGeary,
Rachel Hardwick, Rhiannon Roberts,
Sophie Thomas and Ela Bryan

PUBLISHED BY LLANINA BOOKS

First published in Great Britain in 2010 by
Llanina Books
Plas Llanina
New Quay
Ceredigion SA45 9SJ

ISBN: 978-0-9567 199-0-4

Set in Times and Optima

This book can be ordered at:
www.rogerbryan.com

Printed and bound in Wales at
Gomer Press, Llandysul, Ceredigion, SA44 4JL.

Contents

Foreword

THIS was one of my late mother's favourite sayings along with 'You'll catch your death of cold' and 'There's plenty of room for growth'. This book is full of ideas which, I hope, will indeed 'Come in useful one day'.

It is a personal collection of mnemonics, acronyms, verses, old wives' tales, rhymes, word play and puns, acrostics, images plus a smattering of old jokes, all designed to help you retain and then remember and recall bits of information.

Many were collected over a period of more than 30 years working as a journalist, and others I have created myself. Each entry is aimed at being useful in some situation or other: an examination, an interview, an application for a job, at a dinner party, a pub quiz, an appearance on University Challenge or even Who Wants to be a Millionaire? Indeed as we shall see, it may even help you to keep your job.

I hope that in all possible ways you will find it a book to remember.

Illustrations

Michael Heath: cover, p12, p18

Ron McGeary: p29, p67, p91

Rachel Hardwick: p35, p134, p170

Rhiannon Roberts: p96, p113, p143

Sophie Thomas: p41, p71

Ela Bryan: p40, p65, p105, p110, p130, p183

Roger Sims: Morse Code graphics p 174-75

www.rogerbryan.com
www.ronmcgeary.co.uk
www.rachelhardwick.com
www.rhiannonart.co.uk

Acknowledgements

The entries in this book were collected over the last 40 years, during a life mainly spent in journalism. Many mnemonics are in the public domain, and I have created a number of new ones. I have tried to credit previous authors who have written on the subject and apologise in advance if I have made any major omissions.

The book started, literally and figuratively, with the mnemonic The Siege of Sidney Street, the donor of which now lies in The Tomb of the Unknown Sub-editor. Colleagues along the way have made small and probably unknowing contributions. I thank them all.

Two former Fleet Street colleagues have given advice, help and support especially in the latter stages of the book. Roger Sims, who was always available to help, especially on the production side, and Glyn Evans, who helped to sub-edit and proof-read the copy. Many thanks. Also to George Jaworskyj for looking over the scientific chapters.

Staff at Gomer Press were more helpful and supportive then ever, especially Pît Dafis and Gari Lloyd. Thanks again to the National Library of Wales, Aberystwyth, and also the Ceredigion archives office.

Readers will notice the complete absence of a discernable style to the illustrations in the book. This is not surprising as they were done by six people. Michael Heath, the doyen of British cartoonists, did some work for me a while ago, which gave me a fillip when things were getting hard. I am eternally thankful to him. Ron McGeary came in towards the end and was quick, uncomplaining and thoroughly professional. I used the work of two art students, Rachel Hardwick and Sophie Thomas, and also Rhiannon Roberts, a recent graduate.

I willingly plead guilty to using my 10-year-old daughter Ela. She did a very nice job, and had the the added advantage that she was on the premises and cheap. Thanks to them all.

And finally, again, thanks to my long-suffering wife, Bethan, for her patience and Griff for his excellent proof-reading.

CHAPTER 1

Introduction

Mnemonics: *n pl.* (usu. treated as *sing.*) **1** the art of assisting and improving memory, especially by artificial aids, (but not performance-enhancing drugs): **2** a system of precepts intended to aid and improve the memory. [med.L *mnemonicus* f. Gk *mnemonikos*].

From Mnemosyne, daughter of Earth and Heaven whom the Greeks so revered that they made her the goddess of memory. She was the most beautiful of all the goddesses, attracting Zeus himself; their progeny were the Nine Muses, the goddesses of all things creative.

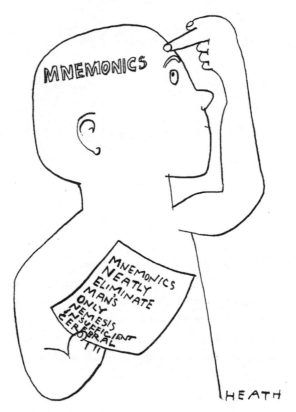

HEATH

Even mnemonics needs a mnemonic to remember how to spell it. It's one of a very small number of words in the English language to start with 'mn', but that may not be enough of a reminder. Here's one:

Mnemonics Neatly Eliminate Man's Only Nemesis: Insufficient Cerebral Storage

Not a good start. It's certainly useful to have a mnemonic mnemonic, but this is not it – you have to know how to spell the word in the first place to get going.

So how about this?

My Nice Editor Measures Out News In Columns

It's shorter, it works and it might just give me (and perhaps you) a leg up sometime in the publishing world.

Mnemonics are reasonably well known to people of a certain age, but fell out of fashion in the 1960s and 1970s.

The late Poet Laureate Ted Hughes blamed it all on the Puritan/Protestant ascendancy in the English Civil War 1642-48 (which is going back a bit to be honest) and the attempt then to banish imagery from all aspects of life.

'The same spirit also banished from the schools the old-established memory techniques that used imagery, and replaced it with learning by rote. The discarded methods were soon forgotten . . . If any attempt was made to reintroduce them, they were dismissed as tricks and cheating'.

A Publisher's Note to A Dictionary of Mnemonics published in 1972 demonstrated the gravity of the situation: 'Times are bad for the memory-aid. Mnemonics were used in Ancient Greece, but today their enemies say that learning from them is like learning about sex from dirty jokes.'

Mnemonics seem to have made something of a comeback recently. So let's come to the aid of the memory aid, with the help of a few (clean) jokes along the way. Let's hear it for the mnemonic.

Perhaps the most famous mnemonic, and certainly one of the best remembered, is the one for the colours of the rainbow …

Richard of York Gave Battle In Vain

Red, Orange, Yellow, Green, Blue, Indigo, Violet.

Millions of children in the UK down the ages have learned the colours of the visible spectrum – the colours of the rainbow – from this, and strangely enough, it appears to be quite popular in the U.S. as well. To me, it has always seemed a very dull mnemonic, albeit an effective one.

So who was Richard of York, and where and in what circumstances did he give battle in vain? One theory has it that it was Richard III, who was defeated in 1485 by Henry Tudor at the Battle of Bosworth Field. This was a major battle that established the Tudor dynasty and ended The War of the Roses. Richard was the Duke of Gloucester, although a member of the House of York.

It seems just as likely that our Richard of York was none other than the Grand Old Duke of York, the one with 10,000 men. Richard Plantagenet, 3rd Duke of York, father of two future kings, Edward IV and Richard III, was defeated and killed at the Battle of Wakefield in The War of The Roses in 1460.

The castle was on top of an old Norman motte and bailey fortress, and after marching his men to the top, where he was impregnable, he was informed that another large column of men was about to relieve him. So he decided to go to engage the enemy, and marched his men back down the hill to join combat against the Lancastrians, only for the Duke and his troops to meet a hasty and nasty end.

So our Richard of York left a grand old legacy . . . a nursery rhyme known by millions:

The Grand Old Duke of York

He had ten thousand men

He marched them up to the top of the hill

And he marched them down again.

When they were up, they were up.

And when they were down, they were down,

And when they were only halfway up

They were neither up nor down.

. . . and one of the most famous mnemonics ever.

Although Richard of York is used in the U.S., the default American mnemonic is:

Roy G. Biv

It's a strange name and Mr Biv (or it could be Mr B the Fourth) hasn't got any of the historical and royal pedigree of our Grand Old Duke, but, well, it works. Even if Biv does mean sewer pipe in Hebrew!

After the Second World War, this one was in circulation in the UK:

Remember O Ye Germans, Britain Is Victorious

And in the 1950s, pupils at a girls' school in York were able to boast:

Rowntrees of York Give Best In Value

Unfortunately, the chocolate and sweet company Rowntrees was later taken over by Nestlé

My favourite was told to me by an Australian sub-editor doing some shifts in Fleet Street:

Rip Out Your Guts Before I Vomit

It's concise and has a graphic Australian directness to it, and I'm sure that it will be met with appreciation and approval by today's teenagers. My teenage son swears by it.

I wanted this to be the title of the book, but friends of mine with more discernment and infinitely better taste advised against it.

THE SIEGE OF SIDNEY STREET

HEATH

CHAPTER 2

Word Pairs

Siege/Seize

The **Si**ege of **Si**dney Street

Once you know this mnemonic, you will never ever misspell siege (or seize) ever again, guaranteed. (This is a non-binding contractual promise on the part of the author). You may not think that this is of much importance, but on a day off when I worked at the London Evening Standard, I was walking down Oxford Street in central London and was mortified to see the banner front page headline on the news-stand with the word

SEIGE

In 108 point type. This is this big.

My first reaction was 'Oh No', and the second was, 'Well, glad I'm on a day off'. It was part of my job to write these headlines, and it doesn't pay to misspell siege (or any other word come to that) in block capitals that are one-and-a-half inches high and read by more than a million people.

I learned this mnemonic back in the 1970s, and it has stuck with me ever since. I think I was told it when I worked on the Yorkshire Post by an old and haggard chain-smoking news sub-editor who had seen better days, but I have never spelled Siege incorrectly since then. Also, I have never heard anyone say the mnemonic, and haven't come across it in any books or on the internet.

So back to the Siege of Sidney Street. For the benefit of younger readers – in this instance, anybody under 90 – this was an incident that took place in the East End of London in 1911. A robbery went wrong and the villains, East European anarchists, fled and ended up in a house in Sidney Street.

The police surrounded the house which then caught fire, and the then Home Secretary, a young Winston Churchill, forbade the Fire Brigade from putting it out. Churchill was later criticised for his intervention, which was widely seen as a publicity exercise.

And for the person who wants to know too much: 20 years later in 1934, Alfred Hitchcock used the siege as the climax of his film The Man Who Knew Too Much.

The mnemonic also applies to seize. Now you know how to spell siege, you know how to spell seize – it's just the opposite of siege.

SEize the day, sail the high **SE**as.

Stationary/Stationery

StationAry:
Imagine that you are on A train in A station, not moving, not going anywhere, you know the sort of thing. You are stationAry.

StatioNEry - think of Notepaper and Envelopes. You are in the station statioNEry shop, thinking of buying Notepaper and Envelopes. You are about to purchase some statioNEry.

Here's a strange thing: have you noticed that on the concourse at all big railway stations, there is a stationery shop? Weird.

Complement/Compliment

Regularly mixed up, especially for some reason on the flyers you get through your door from local takeaways, restaurants, minicab firms and decorators etc. There's generally a complementary half bottle of wine in there somewhere. And also, unforgivably, on menus: the Australian Cabernet Savignon 2007 perfectly compliments the medium-rare kangaroo burger in a koala jus with a julienne of eucalyptus leaves. If only wine bottles could talk.

It's easy – a COMPLEment COMPLEtes.
A compliment doesn't – it is something else – courteous praise.

So a full complement is just that - the complete number of sailors to man a ship for example.
And a full compliment would be something completely different – fulsome praise in fact.

Complementary medicine completes the medical circle. This is correct.

Complimentary medicine is completely different. Instead of saying 'Blimey, you look rough today', the doctor greets you: 'Oh my, you're looking especially healthy today – and I like your jumper too.'

Complimentaries have a separate meaning as freebies.

Practise/Practice
License/Licence

S is the verb, and **C** is the noun
That's the rule that runs the town.

The doctor practises at his Harley Street practice.
The local pub is fully licensed - it has a licence to sell
alcohol.

In the United States, confusingly, it is
the other way round.

Principal/Principle

Principal:
As a noun, treat the princiPAL as your PAL.
As an adjective, treat him as chief

Principle:
None of the above. As a rule, treat it as a the basis of a
moral code.
Your chief friend may be a high principal at the college.
He may, or may not, be a man of high principle,
although we will assume he is.

Effect/Affect

This is a complicated one, because both words serve as nouns and verbs.

To effect means to bring about, to accomplish:
   The win was effected by a late penalty goal.

To affect means to have some influence on something:
   The penalty decision directly affected the outcome of the game.

The effect means the result or consequence of something:
   The effect of the result was that the Rovers stayed top of the table.

The affect is used in psychiatry, quite rare, meaning a mental state or emotion: not to be confused with the effect that watching your football team has on your mental state.

None of this is mnemonic, but you will often see this:

RAVEN
Remember: Affect Verb, Effect Noun

This is wrong, because we know that the two words are both nouns and verbs, but it is as well to know their different meanings.

Stalagmites/Stalactites

An easy one this:

Mites go up and Tites come down.

This is an old fourth-form classic and is still the best for remembering whether stalagmites or stalactites go up from the floor or hang down from the ceiling.

Desert/Dessert

One **S**ugar or two: Twice as much for dessert, only one in the desert.

There/Their

Directions for There
Is it HERE or tHERE?

Ownership for Their
HEIRs inherit tHEIR fortunes.

Ensure/Insure

Ensure is to make certain something happens.
Insure is to buy a policy to protect you from loss, or theft.

An insurance policy was taken out to protect the finances of the village fete in the event of inclement weather: this ensured that the event would not make a loss.

Hypothermia/Hyperthermia

It's important to get this right if you are in the medical profession, not that you wouldn't of course.
Hypo generally means under or below normal
Hypothermia: an abnormally low body temperature.
Hyper generally means over or above normal
and has gained a meaning of excessive. Hyper, hyper
Hyperactive: excessively active, an adjective generally describing a child.

Fewer/Less

This is an important one, as they are quite often used incorrectly in the newspapers and on television. My mnemonic here is neat and concise. Ignore the fact that it is illogical.

Fewer sewers, less mess

Fewer for numbers, less for amount

Quite often wrong at supermarket check-out queues: Less than Five Items is wrong; it should be Fewer than Five Items.

If you can put an ordinal number in front of the noun or pronoun, or the noun/pronoun is a plural, use fewer.
eg seven people, six people, five people, fewer people
eg seven sewers, six sewers, five sewers, fewer sewers

We had fewer cricket matches last summer because of the bad weather.
Less cricket was played last summer because of the bad weather.

The banks had less bad debt than last year.
My son had fewer debts than last year.
(The sentence is correct: would that it were also true!)

Its/It's

This is not a mnemonic, so maybe this should not be here, but it's an important, and short, entry.

Its

means something belongs to someone or something, a possessive.

It's

is a diminution, a shortening, of it is or it has.

Grimethorpe was proud of its mine.
(The pit was in the South Yorkshire town, which was proud both of its mine – and its famous brass band, which also belonged to the town).

Before the coal industry was nationalised in 1947, the colliery owner was able to sing: It's mine, it's mine, it's all mine.

The Greengroce'rs apostrophe:

Generally applied wrongly and needlessly. It denotes a process in which greengrocers, especially those with market stalls, fill up the pepper pot with apostrophes every morning and liberally sprinkle the contents over all their signs. So we get:

APPLE'S, ORANGE'S, BANANA'S,
and POTATO'S, POTATOE'S, POTATOS'
and POTATOES'

where the words are simple plurals and do not need any punctuation.

This incorrect use of the apostrophe was a particular irritant to the master of writing style Keith Waterhouse, who founded the Assocation for the Abolition of the Aberrant Apostrophe more than 20 years ago in the Daily Mail.

He wrote: 'In the AAAA's Black Apostrophe Museum in the basement, which you are welcome to visit, you will find an advertisement from The Guardian for Technical Author's; a circular from the National Council for the Training of Journalists, if you please, containing the phrase "as some editor's will know"; and an announcement from Austin Rover about the new Maestro's.'

Lynn Truss willingly picked up the baton in her 2003 excellent bestseller Eats, Shoots & Leaves.

'No matter that you have a Ph.D and have read all Henry James twice. If you still persist in writing "Good food at it's best" you deserve to be struck by lightning, hacked up on the spot and buried in an unmarked grave.'

In a chapter on apostrophes, she identifies a long list of categories of misuse:

Pupil's entrance (a very selective school)

Giant Kid's Playground (empty – everyone is terrified of the Big Kid).

Cyclist's only (what?)

Childrens education – (in a letter from the head of education at the National Union of Teachers).

The full name and title of person who's details are given in Section 02 – (on UK passport application form).

Gateaux's is just wonderful.

I once noticed at my local municipal sports ground that the bowls were separated into two boxes: bowls and Jack's.

CHAPTER 3

50 Hard Words

Reading reports in the newspapers, it appears that spelling seems to be an increasing problem. In one survey, six out of ten 15-year-olds could not write ten lines without making at least one spelling mistake. And it is not just young people: adults can struggle too. Here are 50 difficult-to-spell words with ways of remembering them.

Separate was adjudged to be the most misspelled word in a survey in 2010. The mnemonics for separate were poor; at least the example below is a great improvement

In his excellent book Every Good Boy Deserves Fudge, Rod L Evans has a section on spelling that contains around 1,000 words. But nobody is going to learn the mnemonics for that number of words. In this instance, less is more.

You can even buy spelling dictionaries (think about it). If you find spelling difficult, my advice would be to buy a medium-sized dictionary which you will find easier to navigate around and just look up any word you are struggling on. For reference, using my Concise Oxford Dictionary, the middle page is M, Magyar in fact. The first quartile almost reached E (dress) and the third quartile started at S (sarong). So if you open the dictionary about halfway, you will be around letter M, and if you open it three-quarters through, you will probably be on letter S.

It is as well to know how to spell. The Spellcheck on the PC is not the answer. A long time ago somebody on the City Desk put in a Spellcheck in an article about merchant bankers Morgan Grenfell which ended up on the page, but not in the paper, as morning greenfly.

This is not a mnemonic, but nonetheless a very important piece of advice that definitely will come in useful:

Always But Always Check Your Written Work, Twice.

Whether it be a letter or an article or an exam paper or anything else. Not checking your work, or least not checking it properly, can have huge consequences for your future career opportunities. Read this cautionary tale.

Robert Barker and Martin Lucas were the Royal printers in London in the early part of the 17th century and publishers of the Bible in 1631 that was to be a reprint of the King James Bible of 1611. They must have wished they had checked their work properly because the Bible became known as the Wicked Bible, or the Sinners' Bible.

The reason was that in Exodus 20:14, a three-letter word was omitted by the compositors. Unfortunately the missing word was 'not' – and even more unfortunately for the printers, it was in the section on the Ten Commandments. The Seventh Commandment now read as an exhortation: 'Thou shalt commit adultery.' Go forth and . . .

The mistake enraged Charles I who ordered the printers to the Star Chamber, where they were fined an amount of money that would have put them out of business; they were deprived of their printers' licence, which did put them out of business; and all the 1,000 Bibles were withdrawn from circulation and burned, although a very small number survived.

Jonathan Franzen, hailed as the new Great American Novelist, encountered a similar problem in 2010 when the British publication of his much-heralded second novel Freedom had to be withdrawn after the printers used an earlier, uncorrected version of the text rather than the final draft. The author spotted hundreds of mistakes in spelling, grammar and characterisation in the first edition.

More than 8,000 books had been sold, which were then withdrawn. Another 80,000 books had already been printed. This is a cautionary tale for anybody who has written a document with multi-versions. You must check and check again that you are working with the right document.

It can't have done anything for Mr Franzen's humour that his much-acclaimed first novel was called The Corrections.

Acceptable
I will accept any table

Accessible
I am always accessIble, I am

Accommodation
ACCoMModation:
Comfy Chairs Only, Many Mod-cons

Address
A double D concerning double S

Aero plane
All Engines Running OK

All right
Alright is alwrong

Apparent
Clearly, A Pushy Parent

Argument
Don't argue – there's no e

Arithmetic
A Rat In The House
Might Eat The Ice Cream

Assassin
The SS strike twice

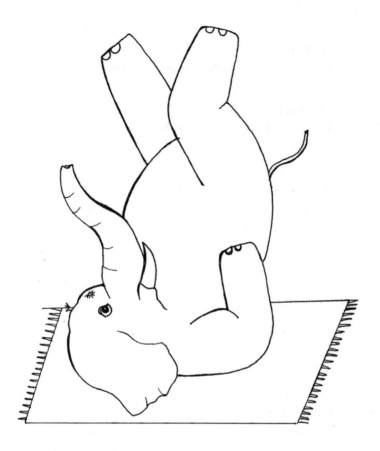

Beauty
Big Elephants Are Usually Trying Yoga

Because
Betty Eats Cheese And Usually Some Eggs. From my youngest daughter, who says she finds it very useful.

Believe
Don't beLIEve a LIE

Benefit
Ben E. Fit (Ben E. King's long lost brother)

Broccoli
C.Coli   (E.Coli's long lost brother)

Cemetery
Three eees. You are walking though a cemetery at
night and something jumps out and screams Eeehhh.
Three ees.

Committee
Doubles all round: double M, double T
and double E

ConSCious
Conscious and Self-Conscious

Consensus
By general agreement, think consent. Nothing to do
with the census

Definite
If it's finite, then there is a good chance that it's definite

Desiccate:
Sic Cate has a dry sense of humour

Desperate
Nil DesPERandum
Think PERil

Diarrhoea
Dash In A Real Rush Home - Or Else Accident!

Disappoint
Di's a People's Princess

Ecstasy
No X please, we're ecstatic

Embarrass
Emba went **R**eally **R**ed **A**nd **S**miled **S**hyly

Exceed
Don't exc-eed the sp-eed limit

Friend
Always a FriEND in the END

Gauge
Get A Useful General Estimate

Geography
General Eisenhower's old girl rode
a pony home yesterday

Graffito (pl graffiti)
Two fingers, one toe (keep moving)
Graffiti: Still two fingers, one tea

Grammar
A ram in the mirror – ram/mar

Haemorrhage
Help! An Emergency Most Often Requiring Rapid
Hospital Attention

Harass
Hit And Run donkey

Hypocrisy
Think hypocrite

Indispensable
Only the most Able people are indispensAble (or so
they tell us)

Inoculate
Usually by in-jection

Irresistible
I'm IrresIstIble (yes you are)

Liaison

Lia is on

(for a secret meeting tonight – it's dangerous)

Mediterranean

Terra firma
The sea in the middle of the land, the
Medi-TERRA-nean being a landlocked sea.

Misspell

Think of that nice English teacher Miss Pell

Minuscule

Sounds like i, but it's a u. Think of minus.
Originally meaning a small cursive script, it has now
taken on the meaning of tiny.

In a survey of spelling on internet newsgroup sites,
minuscule was the word most often spelled incorrectly
– 68% of the time.

It comes from the Latin minusculus meaning rather
less.

Necessary

One collar, two sleeves is needed

Noticeable

You are able to see the notice

para**ll**e**l** **l**ines

Parallel
Parallel lines; four ls

Privilege
Privilege can be judged to be vile

Psycho
Please Send Your Cards Home Often

(So we can keep track of where you are, you nutcase).

I just can't read Psychotherapist as anything other than Psycho The Rapist. Perhaps I need treatment? So will you now.
And watch out for his long-lost brother Hypno the Rapist, who is a very dangerous sort.

Rhythm:
Rhythm Has Your Two Hips Moving

SePARate:
Pull them aPARt
Keep them aPARt
SePARate them, Mum.

In a recent survey, this was the word misspelled the most. This mnemonic here should do the job. The standard mnemonic for remembering how to spell Separate is: Remember it contains a rat. I don't get it.

Vacuum
V double U, nice cars to clean

i before e, except after c

This is a pretty general rule only.

There is an addendum to this:

Or when sounded a
as in neighbour and weigh.

And weird is just weird.

This is a well-known mnemonic, owing its popularity to its brevity as much as anything, and indeed is the title of a recent book on the subject of mnemonics. In practice, there are more than 100 exceptions to the rule, among them:

Neither, either, forfeit, eight, height, protein, seize, science, ancient, efficient, beige, reign, foreign, weight, caffeine, freight, leisure, reindeer, sovereign, et al.

It has been calculated (by whom, I know not) that the i before e rule applies to only 11 out of the 10,000 most common words in English.

The ten most common words in most languages make up 25% of everything we say, so if you're learning a foreign language, it's probably a good idea to learn them, if you don't know them already:

The, be (am, is, are), to, if, and, a(n), in, that, have (has, had), I (me).

In most languages, half of all conversation is made up of 100 words.

Plurals of words ending in o

For a word ending in o preceded by a vowel,
   add S
For a word ending in o preceded by a consonant,
   add ES
For a word relating to music and ending in o,
   add S

Eg: video, videos; radio, radios; stereo, stereos.
   potato, potatoes; tomato, tomatoes;
   piano, pianos; solo, solos; piccolo, piccolos.

When I started to learn Welsh a couple of years ago, I complained to my (Welsh) brother-in-law about how difficult it was. He then emailed me this poem, saying it was lucky I did not have to learn English as a foreign language. I think he had a point.

I take it you already know,
Of *tough* and *bough* and *cough* and *dough*?
Others may stumble, but not you,
On *hiccough, thorough, lough and through*.
Well done. And now you wish, perhaps,
To learn of less familiar traps.
Beware of *heard,* a dreadful *word,*
That looks like *beard* and sounds like *bird*
And *dead*: it's *said* like *bed*, not *bead,*
For goodness' sake, don't call it *deed*.
Watch out for *meat* and *great* and *threat*
They rhyme with *suite* and *straight* and *debt*.
A *moth* is not a *moth* in *mother*
Nor *both* in *bother, broth* in *brother*
And *here* is not a match for *there*
Nor *dear* and *fear* for *bear* and *pear*.
And then there's *dose* and *rose* and *lose*–
Just look them up – and *goose* and *choose*
And *cork* and *work,* and *card* and *ward,*
And *font* and *front,* and *word* and *sword*.
And *do* and *go,* and *thwart* and *cart*.
Come, come, I've hardly made a start.
A dreadful language! Man Alive!
I'd mastered it when I was five.

CHAPTER 4

Numbers

This is the dumbest mnemonic in the book, so here it is at the start of this chapter to get it out of the way. It is a mnemonic for the first ten integers:

Only The Truly Forgetful Fellow Should
Summon Each Number Thusly

Some saddo somewhere spent a fair amount of time thinking up that one. Sorry, ignore the mnemonic and just remember
1, 2, 3, 4, 5, 6, 7, 8, 9, 10

If you need a mnemonic to remember these numbers, you are reading the wrong book.

Square roots

The number of letters in each word represents a digit

I wish I knew – the root of two
1.414

O procure for me – the root of three
1.732

So we can arrive – at the root of five
2.236

We need more logistics – for the root of six
2.449

It rhymes with 'eaven – the root of seven
2.645

Pythagoras's Theorem

For finding the length of the sides of a right-angled triangle

A squared + B squared = C squared
Where A and B are the short sides of the triangle, and C is the Hypotenuse (longest side)

The sum of the square on the hypotenuse is equal to the sum of the squares on the other two sides.

The mnemonic for this is an old school favourite. I can't remember many laughs in maths lessons when I was at school; in fact, this was probably the only one. Here goes:

A Red Indian chief (you can tell how old the story is) had three squaws, all of whom were about to give birth. He laid one squaw on a bear hide; the second squaw on a lion hide; and the third he laid out on a hippopotamus hide.

When they went into labour, the mother on the bear hide gave birth to a son. Soon after, the mother on the lion hide also gave birth to a son. Finally the squaw laid out on the hippopotamus hide gave birth to twin boys. So…

The sons of the squaw on the hippopotamus are equal to the sons of the squaws on the other two hides.

The Metric system

King Hector Doesn't
Usually Drink Cold Milk

Kids Hate Doing Maths
During Cloudy Mondays

Kilo, Hecto, Deca, (unit metre), Deci, Centi, Milli

For the larger metric system:

Good Models Know How Dunkin (units)
Donuts Can Make U Not Petite Females

Giga	10^9	Centi	10^{-2}
Mega	10^6	Milli,	10^{-3}
Kilo,	10^3	Micro	10^{-6} (one millionth)
Hecto	10^2	Nano	10^{-9}
Deca	10^1	Pico	10^{-12} (one trillionth)
Unit		Femto	10^{-15} (one quadrillionth)
Deci	10^{-1}		

(Greek character mu for micro represented by U in mnemonic because it looks like a capital U).)

Roman numerals

Lucy Can't Drink Milk

L = 50
C = 100
D = 500
M = 1,000

Intra-Venous X-ray:

I = 1
V = 5
X = 10

When left is small and right is bigger
Subtract the left from the right-hand figure.
Eg IV   (1 subtracted from 5) = 4
    IX   (1 subtracted from 10) = 9
MCMLIX = 1000 + [1000 – 100] + 50 + [10 – 1].
1959 – a good year, my wife was born.

What number do you get if you add up all the Roman
numerals in order? M D C L X V I = 1666, the year of
the Great Fire of London, I include this only because I
have been told it is a popular pub quiz question.

Map-reading

Read the a X co-ordinates first, then the Y vertical grid. eg a map reading of 123456, read 123 along the bottom and then 456 up the side.

Onwards and upwards

Come in the door before going upstairs.
— Army recruit instruction on how to give map references.

Sines and Cosines

These trigonometric functions are used to relate the angles of a triangle to the length of its sides.

Sines = Opposite/ Hypotenuse
Cosines = Adjacent, /Hypotenuse
Tangent = Opposite/Adjacent

SOH-CAH-TOA (sounds like Krakatoa)

Sailors Often Have
Curly Auburn Hair
Till Old Age

Smiles of Happiness
Come After Having
Tankards of Ale

Multiplying + and – Numbers

This is a multiplication morality tale courtesy of Rod Evans in Every Good Boy Deserves Fudge.

Positive number x positive number = positive number
Positive number x negative number = negative number
Negative number x positive number = negative number
Negative number x negative number = positive number

3 x 4 = 12. 3 x -4 = -12. -3 x 4 = -12. -3 x -4 = 12

If a good thing happens to a good person, that's good.
If a good thing happens to a bad person, that's bad.
If a bad thing happens to a good person, that's bad.
If a bad thing happens to a bad person, that's good.

Also:
Minus x minus is plus
The reason for this we need not discuss.

Even times even is even
Odd times even is even
But odd times odd
Is always odd.

Order of mathematical calculation

PEMDAS
Please Excuse My Dear Aunt Sally

Parentheses, Exponents, Multiplication, Division, Addition, Subtraction

Calculate things in Parentheses first, then square roots and powers etc (Exponents), then Multiply and Divide, and lastly Add or Subtract.

BODMAS

Brackets, Orders, Division, Multiplication, Addition, Subtraction.
(Orders means exponents, and multiplication and division are interchangeable).

In the U.S. brackets are parentheses, so the mnemonic is PODMAS

And in Canada, they call brackets brackets, and exponents exponents, so the
mnemonic is BEDMAS

The Fibonacci Sequence

The Fibonacci Numbers Sequence works like this:

1 + 2 = 3

2 + 3 = 5

3 + 5 = 8

5 + 8 = 13

8 + 13 = 21

13 + 21 = 34

21 + 34 = 55

34 + 55 = 89

Add the last two numbers together to get the next, and so on.

1,1, 2, 3, 5, 8, 13, 21, 34, 55, 89, 144, 233, 377, 610, 987, 1597, 2584, 4181, 6765, 10946 and so on.

Signor Fibonacci, properly Leonardo da Pisa, was born in 1175 to a merchant who later became a customs officer. He travelled widely, and introduced the Latin-speaking world to the decimal number system in his book Liber Abaci. He is best known for this simple series of numbers – the Fibonacci Numbers named in his honour.

The ratio of each pair of Fibonacci numbers 5/3; 8/5; 13/8; 21/13 etc approaches a constant - 1.6180339 and is called the Golden Ratio and Golden Number known simply as phi, and has numerous applications in nature and science.

The Golden Ratio describes a rectangle where the longer side is phi times (1.618) longer than the shorter side.

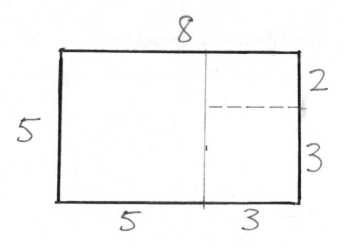

If the rectangle was 8cm long and 5cm on the shorter side it would form a Golden Rectangle (8/5 = 1.6). It can be divided into a square (of 5cm) and a rectangle of 5cm by 3cm, which is also in the proportion of the golden ratio.

There have been many references to the Sequence through history: the Parthenon was said to have been designed on the Golden Ratio principle. How many are true is not known, but the pattern does occur in nature – sunflower seeds in the centre of the flower grow in formations of 55 clockwise and 89 anticlockwise, both Fibonacci numbers. The dimensions of the screen of the Mac laptop I am writing this on are almost the same as the Golden Ratio, as are a standard postcard and a 35mm photographic negative. And also this book laid on its side.

For some reason the Sequence is very useful in changing kilometres into miles. So 55 kilometres equals 34 miles, and 55 miles equals 89 kilometres. 21 miles equals roughly 34 km under the system. The exact figure is 33.79km. 89 km equals roughly 55 miles in the system. The exact figure is 55.30 miles

The Fib system can also be used to convert figures that are not in the series. This is for the more advanced Fibonacci student, but perseverance will get you through.

Take 50 miles for instance. First break down 50 to Fib numbers and multiply through:
21 times 2, add 8. Move one level up the Fib System, and you get
34 times 2 plus 13 = 81 km
(34 follows 21 in the system, and 13 follows 8).
80km is a common speed limit in France.

Going the other way, 13 times 6 plus 2 = 80. Moving one level down the Fib System, this becomes 8 times 6 plus 1 = 49 mph.

A new form of poetry – the fib – has been developed on the internet, generally a six line 20 syllable poem based on the Fibonacci Numbers. The number of syllables in each successive line is the sum of the two previous numbers – 1,1,2,3,5,8.

One
And
Two and
Three and four.
Quick, quick! Close the door.
Before the fibbers call the law.

Haikus they ain't.

Miles and kilometres
5 and 8

One kilometre is 0.6214 of a mile.

Miles to kilometres: divide by 5 and multiply by 8
10 miles is 16 km

Kilometres to miles: divide by 8 and multiply by 5.
24 km is 15 miles.

The number of kilometres is always more than miles because kilometres are shorter than miles.

This is a simple conversion and appears to be fairly accurate.

Pints and Litres
4 and 7

One pint is 568 millilitres.
or 0.568 of a litre.

Pints to Litres:
multiply by 4 and divide by 7

Litres to Pints:
multiply by 7 and divide by 4

Gallons and Litres
9 and 2

Gallons to Litres:
Multiply by 9, divide by 2

Litres to Gallons:
Multiply by 2, divide by 9

A pint's a pound in America all round,
But a pound and a quarter of British water.

An Imperial liquid pint is 20 fluid ounces, and American
pint, 16 fl oz.

Spoons:

One big T equals teaspoons three
One tablespoon (15ml) equals three teaspoons (5ml).
In the U.S., the exact volume of a teaspoon is
4.92892159 ml.

Depth of a Fathom:

Six letters,
Six feet

Mark Twain took his pen name from the word for two
fathoms (twain), the minimum navigable depth of the
Mississippi, where he worked at one time piloting
riverboats.

Billions and trillions

This is not a mnemonic, but knowing these big numbers could be mighty useful one day. It's hard to believe, but until around 35 years ago, Britain and the United States had differing definitions of what constituted a billion and a trillion. Historically, such numbers were not often met with outside of the world of mathematics and science

A million seemed to be OK, six noughts, but that's where the agreement ended. Rather worryingly for the international banking system, the US billion was a thousand million (nine noughts) while in Britain billion had meant a million million (12 noughts). Keep up at the back.

It is a testimony to something that the system carried on working despite a discrepancy of a factor of 1000.

The change in the British definition of a billion came in the Budget statement in 1975 by Chancellor of the Exchequor Denis Healey who announced that the Treasury would from then on adopt the American version.

Apparently, the popular scientist Carl Sagan also helped in the process of change when he announced that in his series of TV lectures at the time, he would use the word billion in its American sense.

The same change affected trillion. The U.S. trillion was a million million, whereas the British version was a million million million. This has now been standardised and a trillion is a million million (12 noughts).

To recap
a million is 6 noughts 1,000,000
a billion is 9 noughts, a thousand million
a trillion is 12 noughts, a million million

The Nine Complement

This is a wonderful numbers game, guaranteed to break the ice at parties. In this instance, the nine complement is the number that needs to be added to another to make 999.

Ask someone for a number between 1 and 999

567

Ask them for another

382

Then repeat the first number

567

and then give your own number. This will be the nine complement of 382 – in this instance 617. Added together the two numbers make 999.

The calculation you are going to do is this:

(567 x 382) plus (567 x 617)
216,594 + 349,839 = 566,433

The quick way goes like this:

567 minus one

566

The nine complement of 566

433

Answer **566,433**

Go on then, check it out.

And try this one

(287 x 748) + (287 x 251)

287 minus 1

286

The nine complement of 286

713

Answer **286,713**
Magic

CHAPTER 5

Times Tables

Two times table:

02, 04, 06, 08, 10

12, 14, 16, 18, 20

2,4,6,8

Two, do we enumerate.

Three times table:

1 x 3	= 3	3	7 x 3	= 21 (2+1)	3
2 x 3	= 6	6	8 x 3	= 24	6
3 x 3	= 9	9	9 x 3	= 27	9
4 x 3	= 12 (1+2)	3	10 x 3	= 30	3
5 x 3	= 15 (1+5)	6	11 x 3	= 33	6
6 x 3	= 18 (1+8)	9	12 x 3	= 36 (3+6)	9

In the four groups of three numbers 1,2,3; 4,5,6; 7,8,9; 10,11,12; the sum of each answer in each group has a pattern of 3,6,9. This simple pattern only works up to 12x3, but there are other more complex patterns after that. This is probably not the place to go into them.

Four times table:

If you struggle here, it's probably best to multiply by two, and then again, and add them up. All products will be even numbers.

1x4 = 2+2 = 4   (1 x 2 = 2, and again, 2: 2 + 2 = 4)

2x4 = 4+4 = 8   (2 x 2 = 4, and again, 4: 4 + 4 = 8)

3x4 = 6+6 = 12   (3 x 2 = 6, and again, 6: 6 + 6 = 12)

4x4 = 8+8 = 16   (4 x 2 = 8, and again, 8: 8 + 8 = 16)

5x4 = 10 +10 = 20

Five times table:

5, 10, 15, 20, 25, 30, 35, 40, 45, 50

Odd numbers x 5 end in 5

Even numbers x 5 end in 0

Six times table:

A similar pattern to the three times table.

$$1 \times 6 = 6 \qquad 6$$

$$2 \times 6 = 12 \qquad 3$$

$$3 \times 6 = 18 \qquad 9$$

$$4 \times 6 = 24 \qquad 6$$

$$5 \times 6 = 30 \qquad 3$$

$$6 \times 6 = 36 \qquad 9$$

$$7 \times 6 = 42 \qquad 6$$

$$8 \times 6 = 48 \qquad 3^* \ (4+8=12: \ 1+2=3)$$

$$9 \times 6 = 54 \qquad 9$$

$$10 \times 6 = 60 \qquad 6$$

$$11 \times 6 = 66 \qquad 3^* \ (6+6=12: \ 1+2=3)$$

$$12 \times 6 = 72 \qquad 9$$

In the four groups of three numbers 1,2,3; 4,5,6; 7,8,9; 10,11,12; the sum of each answer in each group has the pattern 6,3,9

Seven times table:

There doesn't appear to be any shortcuts or patterns to this one: you will have to learn the seven times table by rote (as you should have the others).

You might find it useful to multiply by 5, multiply by 2, and then add them up.

5 x 7 = 5 x 5 (25) + 5 x 2 (10) = 35

Eight times table:

If this causes trouble

Double, double, double

3 x 8 = 24

double   3 = 6

double   6 = 12

double 12 = 24

12 x 8 = 96

double 12 = 24

double 24 = 48

double 48 = 96

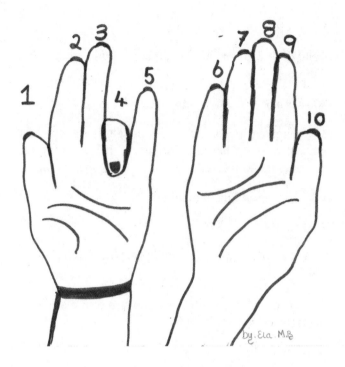

Nine times table:

Open hands out and number left hand

digits from thumb 1,2,3,4,5 and right hand

digits from little finger 6,7,8,9,10.

Eg: 4 x 9

Bend digit 4 down. To the left of it are 3 digits, to the right 6 digits

Answer **36**

Eg: 7 x 9

Bend digit 7 down. To the left are 6 digits, to the right 3 digits.

Answer **63**

My daughter, loved this – she thought it was the best present we gave her last Christmas. It always works, and only needs the ability to count from one to ten.

It still works at bigger numbers

Eg 14 x 9

10 x 9 (right thumb down, **9** to the left, **0** to the right) = **90**

4 x 9 (Fourth finger left hand down, **3** to the left, **6** to the right) = **36**

90 + 36 = **126**

Eg 452 x 9

Split the calculation up.

400 x 9 = **3600**

50 x 9 = **450**

2 x 9 = **18**

3600 + 450 + 18 = **4068**

The nine times table throws up a number of interesting patterns

1 x 9 = 9	5 x 9 = 45	9 x 9 = 81
2 x 9 = 18	6 x 9 = 54	10 x 9 = 90
3 x 9 = 27	7 x 9 = 63	11 x 9 = 99
4 x 9 = 36	8 x 9 = 72	12 x 9 =108

The first five answers are mirrored by the next five:

09, 18, 27, 36, 45

90, 81, 72, 63, 54

And all the products add up to 9. This goes for any number.

Eg 3 x 9

Answer **27** (2+7 = 9)

Eg: 7 x 9

Answer **63** (6 + 3 = 9)

Eg: 28 x 9

Answer **252** (2+5+2 = 9)

Eg: 67452 x 9

Answer **607068** (6+7+6+8 = 27: 2+7 = 9)

Eg: 7683451 x 9

Answer **69151059** (6 + 9 + 1 + 5 + 1 + 5 + 9 = 36: 3 + 6 = 9)

It really does work:

Eg: 8,356,241,890 x 9: That's more than 8 billion!

Answer **75,206,177,010**   (7+5+2+6+1+7+7+1 = 36: 3+6 = 9)

And how's this for a pretty pattern?

$$1 \times 9 + 9 = 18$$
$$12 \times 9 + 9 = 117$$
$$123 \times 9 + 9 = 1116$$
$$1234 \times 9 + 9 = 11115$$
$$12345 \times 9 + 9 = 111114$$
$$123456 \times 9 + 9 = 1111113$$
$$1234567 \times 9 + 9 = 11111112$$
$$12345678 \times 9 + 9 = 111111111$$

Ten times table:

If you can't do the 10 times table, you are probably not going to have understood any of the foregoing, never mind the 11 and 12 times tables still to come. In fact, can you give the book back to your mummy?

Eleven times table:

The only things that I can think of that are counted out in 11s are the number of players in football, cricket and hockey teams and the number of players on the field at any one time for each team in American Football.

A penalty kick in football is taken from a spot 12 yards from the goal: in Germany, a penalty kick is called an Elfmeter – it is approximately 11 meters from the goal (10.9728m to be precise).

The 11 times table is very interesting. It's pretty straightforward up to 9

$11 \times 2 = 22$

$11 \times 3 = 33$

$11 \times 4 = 44$

etc

It gets more interesting - but just as easy - after that:

Eg 12 x 11 The first number **1**

then add the first two numbers (1 + 2) **3**

Then the second number **2**

Answer **132**

Eg 18 x 11

The first number **1**

Add the first two numbers 1+ 8 **9**

Then the last number **8**

Answer **198**

Eg: 153 x 11

The first number **1**

Add the first two numbers (1 and 5) **6**

Add the next two numbers (5 and 3) **8**

Then the last number **3**

Answer **1683**

Eg: 1345 x 11

14795

(1, 1+3, 3+4, 4+5, 5)

When two numbers added together make 10 or more, just carry it over as in any addition.

Eg 13562 x11

1

1+3 = **4**

3+5 = 8 (+1) = **9**

5+6 =11 (this turns the 8 above into 9) remainder **1**

6+2 = **8**

2

Answer **149182**

This a strange thing I found on the internet: Take any number: write if forwards and then backwards:

456 654

This will be a multiple of 11.

41514 x 11

(using the method we have just learnt).

4 5 6 6 5 4

Twelve times table:

Both the 11 times and 12 times tables have lost some of their relevance in these decimal days. There are no longer 12 pennies in a shilling, but there are 12 inches in a foot, eggs are still sold in dozens, there are 12 hours on a clock face, 12 months in a year, and we still celebrate the Twelve Days of Christmas.

This is still an important table and is another one that is best learnt by heart

The only aid I have seen for the 12 times table is

Multiply by 10, then by 2, and then add up them up.

Eg: 12 x 4

10 x 4 = **40**

2 x 4 = **8**

Answer **48**

Fifteen times table:

An easy one this:

Multiply number by 10

Then multiply number by 5

(Or halve the first number)

Then add them together

Eg: 3 x 15

(3 x 10) **30**

(3 x 5) **15**

= **45**

Eg: 17 x 15

(17 x 10) **170**

+ (170/2) **85**

= **255**

Eg: 2840 x 15

(2840 x 10) = **28400**

+ (28400 /2) = **14200**

= **42600**

 (2840 x 10) = **28400**

+ (2840 x 5) = **14200**

= **42600**

In the second part of the calculation, it will be easier to multiply by 5 in some instances, and to halve the first number in others, especially when the numbers are large. It amounts to the same thing - just choose whatever is easier.

CHAPTER 6

History

This is a long-standing classic rhyme for remembering the The Kings and Queens of England, and if you can be bothered to learn it by rote, it is very useful and very definitely will come in useful one day

Willie, Willie, Harry, Stee,
Harry, Dick, John, Harry Three,
One, Two, Three Neds, Richard Two,
Harry Four, Five, Six. Then who?
Edward Four, Five, Dick the Bad,
Harrys Twain and Ned the Lad.
Mary, Bessie, James the Vain,
Charlie, Charlie, James again,
William and Mary, Anna Gloria,
Four Georges, William and Victoria,
Edward Seventh next, and then
George the Fifth in 1910.
Edward the Eighth soon abdicated
And so a George was reinstated.
After which Elizabeth –
That's all folks, until her death.

House of Normandy: William I (The Conqueror) 1066
– 1087; William II 1087–1100; Henry I 1100 – 1135;
Stephen 1135 – 1154.

House of Plantagenet: Henry II 1154 –1189; Richard I
1189 –1199; John 1199 – 1216; Henry III 1216 –1272;
Edward I 1272 – 1307; Edward II 1307 –1327; Edward III
1327 – 1377; Richard II 1377 – 1399.

House of Lancaster: Henry IV (Duke of Lancaster) 1399
– 1413; Henry V 1413 – 1423; Henry VI 1422 – 1461;
1470 – 1471.

House of York: Edward IV, Duke of York, 1461 – 1483;
Edward V 1483; Richard III 1483 – 1485.

House of Tudor: Henry VII 1485 –1509; Henry VIII 1509
– 1547; Edward VI 1547 – 1553; Mary I 1553 – 1558;
Elizabeth I 1558 – 1603.

House of Stuart: James I 1603 – 1625; Charles I 1625 –
1649.

Commonwealth and Protectorate: 1649 – 1660.

House of Stuart: Charles II 1660 – 1685; James II 1685
– 1688.

House of Orange and Stuart: William III 1689 – 1702,
(his wife Mary II 1689 – 1694); Anne 1702 – 1714.

House of Hanover: George I 1714 –1727; George II 1727
– 1760; George III 1760 – 1820; George IV 1820 – 1830;
William IV 1830 – 1837; Victoria 1837 – 1901.

House of Saxe-Coburg-Gotha:
after 1917, the House of Windsor: Edward VII 1901 – 1910;
George V 1910 – 1936; Edward VIII 1936; George VI
1936 – 1952; Elizabeth II 1952 –

The Royal Houses of England:

No Plan Like Yours To
Study History Wisely

Normandy 1066; Plantagenet 1154; Lancaster
1399; York 1461; Tudor 1485; Stuart 1603 – 1649,
1660 – 1689; Hanover 1714; Windsor 1901 –

Red Rose, White Rose:

The White Rose of York and Yorkshire

W is near Y in the alphabet

The Red Rose of Lancaster and Lancashire

This is the other one.

Henry VIII's wives:

Henry VIII had six wives and this famous rhyme describes their respective fates.

Divorced, beheaded, died
Divorced, beheaded, survived

Catherine of Aragon	m 1509
Anne Boleyn	m 1533
Jane Seymour	m 1536
Anne of Cleves	m 1540
Catherine Howard	m 1540
Catherine Parr	m 1543

Kate and Anne and Jane.
And Anne and Kate (again, again).

Cabal:

An interesting one this - the mnemonic for Charles II's five chief ministers. I can't think of a situation in which it will come in useful, but you never know..

The Shorter Oxford Dictionary has an entry for Cabal dated 1646: a private intrigue of a sinister character formed by a small body of persons. There is another entry dated 1660: a small body of persons engaged in private machination or intrigue.

So it was that in 1670, 24 years after the word had been noted and recorded, Charles II's ministers, viz

Clifford, Arlington, Buckingham, Ashley Cooper and Lauderdale.

signed the Secret Treaty of Dover with France.

The initials of the five ministers' names make up the word Cabal. Spooky.

The British Monarchy: Order of Succession

Charlie Windsor Had A Ball

1 Charles

2 William

3 Harry

4 Andrew

5 Beatrice

Eager Eddie Just Lost All

6 Eugenie

7 Edward

8 James, Viscount Severn

9 Louise (Lady Louise Windsor)

10 Anne

Some interesting ones there: who would have thought that Princess Beatrice of York would be at Number 5? And that Prince Edward's children, James and Louise, would be eight and ninth?

The King of Sweden is 210st in line, and strangely, the Queen's husband, Prince Philip, is 503rd. A namesake of mine, Robin Bryan (who he?), is 516th in line. He must be from the other side of the family – in fact his father was American and his mother was Lady Iris Mountbatten. There is an intriguing-looking character at 1264 in the list – Prince Boris of Bulgaria. The British throne is not going to disappear for lack of qualified candidates for the job.

There are moves afoot however to reform the order of succession. Supporters of change want to give equal rights for women to succeed to the throne, superceding the Act of Settlement 1701.

If the law was changed, it would mean that were the monarch (in reality, the next monarch but one, Prince William) to marry and have a daughter, she would accede to the throne. At present a younger son would have precedent over the older daughter. The legislation would also repeal the laws excluding Catholics or those who marry them from the line of succession.

Geoffrey Robertson, QC, was quoted: 'In order to hold the office of head of state you must be a white Anglo-German Protestant – a descendant of Princess Sophia of Hanover – down the male line on the feudal principle of primogeniture. This is in blatant contravention of the Sex Discrimination Act and the Human Rights Act.' Quite.

Battles:

13B, 14A, 15F:

Bannockburn 1314

Agincourt 1415

Flodden 1513

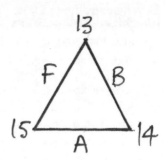

Wars of the Roses:

A Boy Now Will Mention All The Hot, Horrid Battles Till Bosworth

St Albans (1455), Blore Heath, Northampton, Wakefield, Mortimer's Cross, The Second Battle of St Albans, Towton, Hedgeley Moor, Hexham, Barnet, Tewkesbury, Bosworth(1485).

War of the Spanish Succession:

Use the Duke of Marlborough's phone number:

BROM 4689

Blenheim 1704, Ramillies 1706, Oudenarde 1708, Malplaquet 1709.

The Hundred Years' War:

So how long did it last? Correct – 117 years. The mnemonic for this is: add up the number of letters and spaces in Hundred Years' War (17) and add it to the first word you started with, 100. Or conversely, just remember 117. The war between England and France started in 1336 and was deemed to have ended in 1453. The 1000-year Byzantine Empire ended in the same year.

The Spanish Armada:

The Spanish Armada met its fate

In 1500 and 88.

Here's an interesting one – probably the first BOGOF mnemonic: Buy One, Get One Free.

George III said with a smile,

1760 yards in a mile.

George III acceded to the throne in 1760, and there are 1760 yards in a mile. In today's metric world, there may be more schoolchildren who know that George III became king in 1760 than there are those who know how many yards are in a mile.

Oh and the number of feet in a mile:

Five tomatoes: 5 2 8 0

This is an American mnemonic, and so you have to say to-mayt-oes.

A Cat Eats My Hat.

Which Hat, What Cat?

That's My Burmese Blue Cat!

Atlee, Clement	1945-51
Churchill, Winston	1951-1955
Eden, Anthony	1955-1957
Macmillan, Harold	1957-1963
Home, Alec Douglas	1963-1964
Wilson, Harold	1964-1970
Heath, Edward	1970-1974
Wilson, Harold	1974-1976
Callaghan, James	1976-1979
Thatcher, Margaret	1979-1990
Major, John	1990-1997
Blair, Tony	1997-2007
Brown, Gordon	2007-2010
Cameron, David	2010-

At The Canine Club, Never Give Out Vile Vegetables To Dalmatians

Augustus	27BC – AD 14
Tiberius	14 - 37
Caligula	37 - 41
Claudius	41 - 54
Nero	54 - 68
Galba	68 - 69
Otho	69
Vitellius	69
Vespasian	69 - 79
Titus	79 - 81
Domitian.	81 - 96

The Seven Wonders of the Ancient World:

Peggi's Garb, Pal? Color, Temp Def... States Jo (Oz), To mahal.

This is how mnemonics used to be. It will never be one of the wonders of the world and wins the prize for the clunkiest entry, but it does do its job, giving two clues for each wonder. If you can trust this to memory it certainly will come in useful one day

1   Pyramids of Egypt (Giza)

2   Hanging Gardens of Babylon (Baghdad)

3   Pharos of Alexandria

4   Colossus of Rhodes

5   Temple of Diana (Ephesus)

6   Statue of Jupiter (Zeus) at Olympia

7   Tomb of Mausolus (Halicarnassus)

Or try PG: PC, DJ's TM

Parental Guidance: PC, the DJ's Trade Mark

Pyramids, Gardens, Pharos, Colossus, Diana, Jupiter, Tomb of Mausolus.

CHAPTER 7

Geography

North and South

There are two more contenders here for the most simple mnemonic in the book. The first one comes courtesy of Lord Brocket.

The peer was serving five years at Littlehey Prison in Cambridgeshire for attempted fraud. Life inside was tough for a peer of the realm, but in a letter to the novelist Dame Barbara Cartland, he said he had been trying to help some of his fellow inmates, a number of whom were illiterate and innumerate. He said he showed a map of Britain to one inmate, who had no idea what it was.

'As for London, he hadn't a clue. North and South, he had no idea. So I told him:

Nut (Head) for **N**orth and **S**hoes for **S**outh

– and he's got it! Most people won't need a mnemonic for north and south, but full marks to Lord Brocket in coming up with one which was both meaningful and effective in the situation.

Another mnemonic for north and south,

and east and west is:

Never Eat Shredded Wheat

Don't really mean that Nestlé! Shredded Wheat is good for you – it is made from just one ingredient: 100% Whole Grain Wheat. Nothing more. Nothing extra. That should keep the Nestlé lawyers happy.

Left and Right:

Pretty simple stuff I know.

With your left hand face down, move the thumb 90 degrees away from the index finger. You get the shape of a capital L. This is your Left Hand.

The other one is Not Your Left Hand -–The Right Hand.

It's basic I know, but apparently more people than you would think have trouble knowing their right from their left.

It also works in French:

Gauche (Left): make a G with your thumb and first finger on your left hand. Droit (Right) make a D with your thumb and first finger on the right hand

And German: Links (left) and the other one, Recht (right). And it completely works in Welsh, too: Chwith (Left) and De (right).

While we're on the basics, how about this for how to lay the table:

Left......Fork   (4 letters)

Right....Knife (5 letters)

Port and Starboard

We left port and went right to starboard.

There's some more red port left.

Port is left – both have four letters.

Port is always passed to the left round the dinner table

The seven continents:

Eat An Aspirin After
A Night-time Snack

Europe, Antarctica, Asia, Africa,

Australia, North America, South America.

(The second letter in the first three A entries is another clue).

Longitude and Latitude:

LONGitude: Think of great LONG circles running north-south meeting at the Poles. All the circles are the same length. LONGitude is the distance ALONG the Equator measured in degrees from Greenwich

LATitude is the LATeral distance north or south from the Equator measured in degrees. This could be termed lateral thinking, or sideways, across thinking. The circles decrease in size as they move away from the equator towards the poles.

The Equator is at Latitude 0 degrees, and the Poles at Latitude 90 degrees. Greenwich, the home of The Royal Observatory in South East London, is at 0 degrees Longitude, and 51.5 degrees North Latitude.

The Great Lakes:

No collection of mnemonics would be complete without a few concerning the Great Lakes of North America – sometimes I think they are there just to bulk out the collection. So in the interests of comprehensiveness and bulkiness, here they are:

HOMES:

Huron, Ontario, Michigan, Erie, Superior.

West to East:

Susan Mitchell Has Eight Oranges

Superior, Michigan, Huron, Erie, Ontario.

And this taught at the Convent of Sacred Heart High School in Hammersmith, London, in the 1940s:

Some Monkeys Hate Eating Oranges

East to West:

Only Elephants Have Massive Snouts

Ontario, Erie, Huron, Michigan, Superior.

By area:

Sam's Horse Must Eat Oats

Superior, Huron, Michigan, Erie, Ontario.
That's enough Great Lakes – Ed.

Longest rivers:

Rivers change their length all the time, and measuring standards change too, so there is no list that is going to be definitive for ever. When I first wrote this list last year, the Ob-Irtysh was the fifth longest but has now been downgraded to seventh, losing more than 100 miles in the process.

By popular agreement, though, the Nile is the longest river in the world at 4,160 miles. It rises in Burundi and with its tributaries, flows through nine countries before reaching the Nile delta and the Mediterranean. The Amazon is the biggest river in the world measured by the amount of water that flows down it.

NAY.MY.HO

Nile	4,132 miles	6,650km
Amazon	3,976	6,400
Yangste	3,917	6,300
Mississippi	3,902	6,275
Yenisey	3,445	5,539
Huang He	3,398	5,464
Ob-Irtysh	3,364	5,410

No, I'd never heard of the Yenisey or the Ob-Irtysh either. The Huang He is the Yellow River, so-called after the colour of its silt.

All these rivers are just about twice as long as the longest river in Europe, the Danube (1770 miles). The source of the Yenisey is in central Mongolia and flows south to north through Siberia to the Arctic Ocean. The Ob rises in the Altai Mountains and flows through Siberia to the Gulf of Ob. The Irtysh, which originates in China, is its main tributary, and both these rivers are frozen over for half the year.

The UK's longest river is the Severn at 354km, just ahead of the Thames at 346km.

Highest mountains:

EK too

Everest	8,850m
K2	8,610m
Kangchenjunga	8,586m

The oceans:

Perhaps Aunt Ira should call the AA

Pacific, Atlantic, Indian Antarctic, Arctic.

Beverly Hills

Readers will have noticed that the definition of a mnemonic in the book has been pretty wide. Well here's another one.

If we say a mnemonic is an aid to memory, then how about this – the threat of the sack?

When I had a position of some power on a Sunday newspaper, I made a (half-serious) rule that any sub-editor who allowed Beverly Hills to be spelled incorrectly in the newspaper (as Beverley, the spelling of Hills generally not being a problem) would be sacked on the spot.

I don't know why that particular error bugged me so much, but it did. It may have been that there seemed to be a reference to Beverly Hills on every other page (and these days, almost every other story).

But nobody ever did spell it incorrectly, and therefore nobody was ever summarily dismissed. So the threat of the sack proved to be a very effective aid to memory.

In researching this book, I discovered that Beverly Hills, California, was named at the start of the 20th century after the small town of Beverly and its rolling hills in Massachusetts.

And that the settlement of Beverly, Massachusetts, was named in 1668– yes you've guessed it – after Beverley in north Yorkshire.

So Beverly itself was a spelling mistake all along. I feel a bit better now that nobody was fired.

And while we are in West Los Angeles:

Glenn Close:

Two Ns, the same as Bunny Boiler in Fatal Attraction.

And the streets of New York:

Eastbound streets are even,

Westbound streets are odd.

Obey the traffic signals,

And leave the rest to God.

The Seven Hills of Rome:

(Clockwise from the west)

Can Queen Victoria Eat Cold Apple Pie?

Capitoline, Quirinal, Viminal, Esquiline,

Caelian, Aventine, Palatine

Some local mnemonics:

The Rivers of Yorkshire:

Surely Una Never Was A Careful Driver.

Swale, Ure, Nidd, Wharfe, Aire, Calder, Don

Stoke-upon-Trent:

Two Brown Hats Sell For Less

You're not going to get this one easily. It was taught (among other things I'm sure) at Rhondda County Girls School, Porth, in South Wales in the 1960s and is the mnemonic for the six towns that make up Stoke-upon-Trent in Staffordshire. If this comes in useful you must be taking part in a pub quiz in the Potteries.

Tunstall, Burslem, Hanley, Stoke, Fenton, Longton

The counties of Northern Ireland:

FAT LAD

Fermanagh, Antrim, Tyrone, Londonderry, Armagh,Down

CHAPTER 8

The Weather

Red sky at night –
Shepherds' delight.

Red sky in the morning –
Shepherds' warning.

The American version has sailors instead of shepherds, both occupations having good reason to keep a close eye on the weather.

There are a number of old wives' tales relating to the weather but this is really an ancient wives' tale that had been passed on by word of mouth for centuries.

The first written version is in the Wycliffe Bible of 1384 and it appears thus in the King James Authorised

Version of the Bible published in 1611 in the Gospel according to St Matthew, 16:2-3:

[Jesus said unto the Pharisees and the Sadducees]

When it is evening, ye say, It will be fair weather: for the sky is red.

> And in the morning, It will be foul weather to day: for the sky is red and lowring.

Shakespeare noted the phenomenon in his epic poem Venus and Adonis (1593):

> Like a red morn that ever yet betokened,
>
> Wreck to the seamen, tempest to the field,
>
> Sorrow to the shepherds, woe unto the birds,
>
> Gusts and foul flaws to herdmen and to herds.

This is more than an ancient wives' tale, being soundly based on science. The sky is full of dust particles and water droplets that scatter the sun's rays. During the day when the sun is high, the sunlight has to pass through less atmosphere before we see it. The sunlight is scattered more effectively by short wavelengths – which is why the sky is blue

At sunset, when the sun is low on the horizon, the sunllight has to pass through more atmosphere than when the sun is overhead. The shorter wavelengths are filtered out, leaving only the longer wavelengths of red, orange and yellow light for us to see. As the sun sets in the west and our weather generally comes in from the west, if there no clouds in the sky, there is a good chance of clear skies and fine weather ahead.

In the morning, equally, the sun rising in the east has to pass through more atmosphere and when it reflects the water vapour and dust particles of a weather system that has come in from the west, it will be coloured red-ish. A red sky in the morning means that there is a high water content in the atmosphere – and rain is probably on the way.

St Swithun's Day

St Swithin's Day, if thou dost rain,

Full forty days it will remain.

St Swithin's Day, if thou be fair,

For forty days, t'will rain na mair.

St Swithin (properly Swithun), was Bishop of Winchester in the 9th Century and requested to be buried in humble surroundings outside the cathedral so the sweet rain of heaven could fall on him. More than one hundred years later, the monks decided that this was not a fitting resting place for him and arranged to move his remains to a shrine inside the cathedral on July 15, 971.

According to legend, there was a great storm that day and then torrential rain for forty days. Believing that this was evidence of St Swithin weeping in despair, the monks decided against moving his remains. This led to the old wives' tale that if it rained on July 15, it would rain continuously for forty days. And vice-versa.

St Dunstan's Day

Last frosts before summer:

Another old wives' tale involving the weather and a bishop and a saint – in this case St Dunstan. Before he became Bishop of Worcester, and subsequently Archbishop of Canterbury (960 – 978), he set himself up as a brewer in the days when there was much competition between ale producers and cider makers.

A sequence of frost-free springs in Somerset had been a boon for the cider makers. In the face of this he is supposed to have sold his soul to the devil in return for regular May frosts which would kill off the apple blossom, and thus help to kill off the competition to his brewing business. Satan, apparently, agreed to engineer frosts each year between May 17 and May 19, the last being St Dunstan's Day.

To this day, it is not uncommon for the last frosts before summer in lowland southern England to be around these dates.

Another story relates how Dunstan, who had also trained as a blacksmith, hammered a horseshoe into the Devil's hoof when he was asked to reshoe the Devil's horse. This was extremely painful and Dunstan only agreed to remove the shoe after the Devil promised never to enter any place where a horseshoe was over the door – the origin of the lucky horseshoe.

Oak and ash:

If the oak before the ash,

Then we'll only have a splash.

If the ash before the oak,

Then we'll surely get a soak.

This weather folklore, based on when trees come into leaf, may soon become obsolete. Warmer springs are advancing the oak more quickly than the ash. The Woodland Trust reported in 2008 that the ash had come into leaf before the oak only four times since 1964.

Wind:

You always know the way they go

Because they blow from High to Low

Wind blows from High Pressure to Low Pressure:

Warning of rain:

Swallows high, staying dry.

Swallows low, wet twill blow.

It appears that as the weather clears after rain, the insects the swallows feed on dry out their wings better by flying higher. So the swallows fly high to catch them. The insects are also carried higher by the warmer air currents that accompany the dry weather.

And if it is raining or threatening rain, they stay low.

Fishing:

When the wind is in the east / It's neither good for man nor beast.

When the wind is in the north / The skilful fisher goes not forth.

When the wind is in the south / It blows the bait in the fish's mouth.

When the wind is in the west / Then it is at its very best.

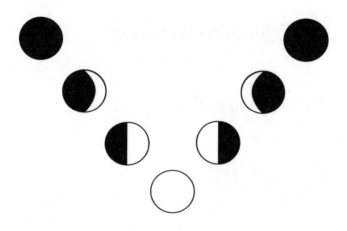

Phases of the Moon

When C is Coming, it's actually going.

When D is Departing, it's actually coming.

.DOC. The phases of the moon: The new moon (nothing), the first quarter getting bigger shaped like D, the second quarter full like O, the third quarter getting smaller shaped like C and the fourth quarter new (nothing).

Predicting the Harvest:

Mist in May, heat in June

Make the harvest come on soon.

Celsius temperatures:

30 is hot, 20 is nice,

10 is cold and 0 is ice.

For those of us who still struggle with the new scale:

Freezing is 0 Celsius, 32 Fahrenheit

Remember 10 Celsius is 50 Fahrenheit.

Two easy ones to flip: 16C is 61F : 28C is 82F

1966 - The unforgettable annus mirabilis for England – the year we won the World Cup. 19C is 66F

20C is 68F.

The formula for converting Fahrenheit to Celsius:

Subtract 32 from the deg F and then multiply by 5/9.

Eg 72F minus 32 = 40 multiplied by 5/9 = 22C

For converting Celsius to Fahrenheit:

Multiply the deg C by 9/5 and then add 32.

Eg 20C times 9/5 equals 36. Add 32. Answer 68F

CHAPTER 9

Time

Spring Forward, Fall Back

This is the failsafe for remembering whether the clocks go forward or back in the spring and autumn.

They spring forward in March (on the last Sunday) and go back in the fall (on the last Sunday) in October.

Despite this simple mnemonic, it is surprising how many people don't know which way the clocks change. (One way round this, of course, is to buy a radio-controlled clock or alarm clock which automatically and quite magically resets the time in spring and autumn).

In March, the clocks change at 01.00 Greenwich Mean Time (because we're on GMT then) and at 02.00 British Summer Time in October, (because we're on BST then).

There has been some support recently for moves to increase the amount of light in the evenings.

It works like this. In the autumn when the clocks would normally fall back to GMT, they wouldn't change.

So we would still be on BST, which is GMT+1.In the spring, the clocks would go forward as normal, and this would be to Double BST (BST+1 or GMT+2).

When it came to the autumn the clocks would go back an hour again – to GMT +1 (or BST).

There's nothing miraculous about this – it's not creating more daylight. What it is doing is using the daylight we get in a more effective and efficient way.

This simply would be the singular, most-happiness inducing legislation that any government could introduce – so it's not going to happen.

Apart from the sheer enjoyment of effectively having an extra hour of sunlight in the evenings, it has been estimated that 150 deaths on the roads would be saved every year. The Royal Society for the Prevention of Accidents estimates that 450 deaths and serious injuries would be prevented annually.

A recent Cambridge University study estimated that electricity use by domestic consumers increased by 5% because of the darker evenings caused by the clock going back, generating millions of tons of carbon dioxide in the process.

Darker evenings mean that crime, especially, burglary, muggings and vandalism, goes up. And the London Chamber of Commerce believes that millions of pounds could be saved by Britain coming into line with Western European time.

So what's not to like?

A scientific friend of mine points out that Co-ordinated Universal Time (UTC) replaced GMT as the main scientific time reference scale in 1972. For the general reader, GMT is the same as UTC.

It came by its abbreviation when the International Telecommunication Union wanted the English CUT to be the universal abbreviation. But the French wanted the abbreviation TUC = Temps Universel Co-ordonne. So in a classic committee compromise, they came up with the abbreviation UTC.

So Double BST is actually UTC+2.

Days in the Month:

Thirty days hath September,

April, June and November.

All the rest have thirty one.

Except for February alone,

Which hath twenty-eight days clear

And twenty-nine in each Leap year.

A famous and useful old rhyme. Incidentally, the extra day in a leap year is in February because that was the last month in the Roman calendar, and was therefore the natural time for them to do their four-yearly temporal housekeeping.

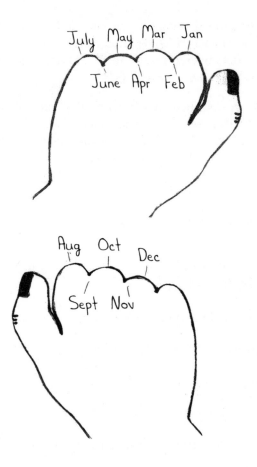

A visual way of remembering the days of the months. Make a fist. Start on the first knuckle and go across the knuckles and spaces in between. A knuckle is 31 days, a dip is 30. After July, go on to the first knuckle of the other hand, which is August. February is 28 or 29. I don't know why it works, but it does.

You do wonder why some mnemonics get written. This one is not as bad as the first ten integers, but it's up there – it's one for the months of the year:

Joan Found Mark And Mike Jumping Janet And Susan Outside Nora's Drugstore

I think it's probably easier just to remember the names of the months.

The Four Seasons:

Their start dates – it's always twentysomething: count the vowels in the season's name for the number.

Spring	(1 vowel)	21 March
Summer	(2 vowels)	22 June
Autumn	(3 vowels)	23 September
Winter	(2 vowels)	22 December

These dates roughly correspond with the dates of the spring and autumn equinoxes, and the dates of the summer and winter solstices, which are approximately on the 21st day of the last month of every quarter.

The equinox is when the sun is directly above the equator, and so the length of day and night are approximately the same.

The solstice is when the tilt of the earth's axis is directly towards and away from the sun, giving us the longest and shortest days of the year.

The Quarter Days:

These roughly coincide with the equinoxes and solstices, each representing a quarter of the year – spring, summer, autumn and winter. The mnemonic is: the number of letters in the month denote the second digit in the 20-something number. Christmas is the exception, most people knowing what day it falls on without a mnemonic.

March	(5 letters)	25	Lady Day
June	(4 letters)	24	Midsummer Day
September	(9 letters)	29	Michaelmas Day
December		25	Christmas Day

The four Quarter Days were part of a list of special days in the Christian Calendar, when among other things, rents and leases were due, taxes were collected and work contracts started and ended.

The Quarter Days were in the news recently. Retailers have been complaining that the practice of quarterly rents dating from the Middle Ages places too large a burden upon them in these straitened times

To help their cash flow, campaigners want landlords to allow retailers to pay rent monthly in advance rather than three months in advance.

In fact, in September 2008, Hermes, one of the biggest property companies in the UK, with holdings of £11bn, broke with tradition to end the historical requirement that the rent be paid quarterly in advance and is to offer its 2,000 tenants more flexible terms.

Signs of the Zodiac:

A Tense Grey Cat Lay Very Low,
Sneaking Slowly, Contemplating A Paw

Aries, Taurus, Gemini, Cancer, Leo, Virgo, Libra,
Scorpio, Sagittarius, Capricorn, Aquarius, Pisces.

This verse is by English preacher and poet Isaac Watts (1674–1748), who wrote more than 700 hymns.

The Ram, the Bull, the heavenly Twins

And next the Crab, the Lion shines,

The Virgo and the Scales,

The Scorpion, Archer and Sea-Goat,

The Man who pours the water out

And Fish with glittering tails.

CHAPTER 10

The Sciences

The speed of light

We guarantee certainty,
clearly referring to this light mnemonic

(Count the letters in each word of the sentence).

299,792,458 metres per second

Which is approximately 186,000 miles per second.

Temperature of Absolute Zero

Soon chill overtakes people totally

Minus 459.67 degrees Fahrenheit

The number of letters in each word gives the answer.

The Periodic Table

A table listing the chemical elements in terms of increasing atomic number which was formalised by the Russian scientist Dmitri Mendeleyev in 1869.

Elements 1 - 10:

Hell, Here Little Beatniks Brandish
Countless Numbers Of Flick kNivEs

Hydrogen, Helium, Lithium, Beryllium, Boron, Carbon, Nitrogen, Oxygen, Fluorine, Neon

H, He, L, Be, B, C, N, O, F, Ne

Elements 11 - 17:

Naughty Maggie Always Sips
Pure Sweet Claret

Na Mg Al Si P S Cl

Sodium, Magnesium, Aluminium, Silicon, Phosphorus, Sulphur, Chlorine

These two short periods can also be remembered by simple abbreviations:

1 – 10: Hhelibeb can of nee

11 – 17: Namgal sips claret

There are at present 118 elements in the Periodic Table. It is interesting to note that Element 117, Ununseptium, symbol Uus, has not yet been discovered.

The order of the Earth's atmospheres

The Strong Man's Triceps Explode

Troposphere, Stratosphere, Mesosphere,
Thermosphere, Exosphere

The electromagnetic spectrum

(From the shortest waves to the longest: the shorter
the wave, the higher the energy).

Cary Grant eXpects Unanimous Votes in Movie Reviews

Cosmic rays

Gamma rays

X-rays

Ultra violet light

Visible light

Infrared

Microwaves

Radio waves

Mohs' Scale of Hardness for minerals:

Those Girls Can Flirt and Other Queer Things Can Do

1 Talc	6 Orthaclase (feldspar)
2 Gypsum	7 Quartz
3 Calcite	8 Topaz
4 Fluorite	9 Corundum
5 Apatite	10 Diamond

The first two can be scratched by a thumbnail. The next four can be scratched by a penknife and the last four will scratch glass. A fingernail has a hardness of 2.5: a 2p piece has a hardness of 5.5. Each mineral can scratch another with a lower Mohs' number

I assumed Mohs was an acronym for Measure of Hardness Scale. In fact Herr Friederich Mohs was born in 1773 with this presciently appropriate surname: he became a German minerologist of note and gave his name to the scale which he codified around 1800 and which is still in use today.

Geological time periods

Camels Often Sit Down Carefully.
Perhaps Their Joints Creak?
Persistent Early Oiling Might Prevent
Permanent Rheumatism

Cambrian, Ordovician, Silurian, Devonian,
Carboniferous, Permian, Triassic, Jurassic,
Cretaceous, Palaeocene, Eocene, Oligocene, Miocene,
Pliocene, Pleistocene, Recent (Holocene).

Order of the biological groupings in taxonomy

King Philip Came Over For Good Sex

Keep Ponds Clean Or Fish Get Sick

Kingdom, Phylum, Class, Order, Family, Genus,
Species

The five classes of vertebrate animals

FARM-B:

Fish, Amphibians, Reptiles, Mammals, Birds.

The first three are cold-blooded, the last two warm-blooded.

Nerves:

On Old Olympus's Towering Tops,
A Finn and German Viewed Some Hops

Olfactory, optic, oculomotor, trochlear, trigeminal, abducens, facial, auditory, glossopharyngeal, vagus, spinal accessory, hypoglossal.

Branches of facial nerve:

Two Zebras Bought My Car

Temporal, Zygomatic, Buccal, Mandibular, Cervical

Nerves in superior orbital tissue of skull:

This next one gets in solely for the mnemonic, not the subject matter.

Lazy French Tarts Lie Naked
In Anticipation

Lacrimal, Frontal, Trochlear, Lateral, Nasociliary, Internal, Abduceir.

Bones:

Spinal Column:

Clever Tom Looks Silly Clot

Cervical, Thoracic, Lumbar, Sacrum, Coccyx.

Arm:

Some Crooks Have Underestimated
Royal Canadian Mounted Police.

Scapula, Clavicle, Humerus, Ulna, Radius, Carpals,
Metacarpals, Phalanges.

Leg:

Help Five Police To Find
Ten Missing Prisoners

Hip, Femur, Patella, Tibia, Fibula, Tarsals,
Metatarsals, Phalanges.

The wrist: (carpals)

Some Lovers Try Positions
That They Can't Handle

Scaphoid, Lunate, Triquetrum, Pisiform,
Trapezium, Trapezoid, Capitate, Hamate.

There are two rows of four carpals each. The list goes
left to right from Scaphoid, and then in the second row,
left to right from Trapezium. This is for a right hand,
palm down.

The skull:

Old People From Texas Eat Spiders

Occipital, Parietal, Frontal, Temporal, Ethmoid,
Sphenoid

The three main insect body parts:

HAT

Head, abdomen, thorax

(Not in order!)

Optics:

The additive and subtractive mixtures of colours:

Better Get Ready While
Your Mistress Comes Back

Blue + Green + Red = White (additive)

Yellow + Magenta + Cyan = Black (subtractive)

For the oscillation of a pendulum:

The wonders of Nature, quoth he

Are always a marvel to me:

That each tick and a tock

of a grandfather clock

is two pi root l over g

Where T = period of the pendulum

l = the length of the pendulum

g = acceleration due to gravity.

The APGAR Score:

Devised in 1952 by Canadian paediatrician Dr Virginia Apgar as a simple method to quickly assess the health of babies immediately after childbirth.

Appearance (skin colour)

Pulse

Grimace (reflex irritability)

Activity (muscle tone)

Respiration

There are two marks in each category, and so a perfectly healthy new born baby will get a score of 10. Strangely, the APGAR score also works in French, German and Spanish.

Resistor colour codes:

Electronic resistors have coloured bands on them to denote their level of resistance on a scale from 0 – 9:

Black, Brown, Red, Orange, Yellow, Green, Blue, Violet, Grey, White.

Bad Boys Rough Our Young Girls, But Violet Goes Willingly.

Better Be Ready, Or Your Great Big Venture Goes West.

(from an old Boy Scout Book on electricity).

Bye Bye, Rosie. Off You Go: Birmingham via Great Western

Ohm's Law:

Virgins Are Rare

Volts = Amps x Resistance

True direction:

For converting compass headings back to true ones:

Cadbury's Dairy Milk   Very Tasty

Compass + Deviation = Magnetic + Variation = True

(Taught at Air Navigation School, RAF Cottesmore in 1942)

For converting true directions to compass readings:

True Virgins Make Dull Company

True +Variation = Magnetic + Deviation = Compass

Acid tests:

May her rest be long and placid

She added water to the acid

The other girl did what she oughta

She added acid to the water.

Johnny was a scientist, Johnny is no more.

For what he thought was H_2O was H_2SO_4.

Sulphuric acid (H_2SO_4) must be poured into water. The other way round is dangerous and could prove fatal. H_2SO_4 certainly should not be drunk.

CHAPTER 11

Astronomy

The Harvard Spectral Classification of Stars:

(Stars in descending order of surface temperature).

O B A F G K M.RNS

Oh Be A Fine Girl, Kiss Me
Right Now, Sweetie

Originally the scheme used capital letters running alphabetically, but was later reordered to reflect the surface temperatures. The stars are classified into different types, O B A etc, where each star type is cooler than the previous. O-type stars are blue and hot (c 35,000C) and shine with the power of 1million times the Sun's output. Our Sun is a classified as a G star.

RN and S type-stars are cooler but can be added to the classification as can L and T stars, which are brown dwarfs.

O B A F G K M .LT

Officially, Bill Always Felt Guilty
Kissing Monica Lewinsky Tenderly

Henry Norris Russell, the leading theoretical American astronomer of his time, is credited with the original mnemonic, which must have upset many thousands of female students through the years. The alternative is:

Oh Be A Fine Girl,
Kiss Me Right Now...Smack

The five brightest stars:

Sirius, Canopus, Alpha Centauri, Arcturus, Vega.

Some Constellations
Actually Aid Vegans

Sirius is twice as bright as any other star in the sky. It is part of the Canis Major constellation and is sometimes called the Dog Star. In ancient Greek times, the dawn rising of Sirius marked the hottest part of the summer, and is thought to be origin of the phrase the dog days of summer. Alpha Centauri is visible only in the southern hemisphere.

Order of the Planets:

Mercury, Venus, Earth, Mars, Jupiter, Saturn, Uranus, Neptune, Pluto

My Very Easy Method.
Just Set Up Nine Planets

Pluto was demoted from full planetary status in 2006. An American website held a competition for the best new mnemonic, and the winner was:

My! Very Educated Morons Just
Screwed Up Numerous Planetariums

Other new ones without Pluto are:

My Very Easy Method: Just SUN

Pluto was discovered in 1930 by Percival Lowell – Pl – and this doleful mnemonic was written for him. A favourite:

My Vision, Erased. Mercy! Just

Some Underachiever Now.

Distance of the Planets to the Sun:

In the following scale, £1 equals one astronomical unit, ie the mean distance from the Earth to the Sun, about 93 million miles.

Mercury	39p
Venus	72p
Earth	£1.00
Mars	£1.50
Jupiter	£5.20
Saturn	£9.50
Uranus	£19.00
Neptune	£30.00

Size of Planets:

Sun – J – Sun

Sun, Jupiter, Saturn, Uranus, Neptune.

For information, the different orders of size are: 865, 89, 75, 32, 30

CHAPTER 12

Religion

Books in the Bible:

Old Testament:

3 letters and 9 letters gives 39

New Testament:

3 letters times 9 gives 27

The Twelve Disciples:

This is the way the disciples run.

Peter, Andrew, James and John,

Philip and Bartholomew,

Thomas next and Matthew, too,

James the less and Judas the greater,

Simon the zealot and Judas the traitor.

The Ten Commandments:

One idle damn Sunday, Dad killed
cheating thief and lied to cover it

No other Gods, no idols, don't blaspheme, rest on the
Sabbath, respect your parents, don't kill, don't commit
adultery, don't steal, don't bear false witness and don't
covet.

The Ten Plagues of Egypt:

Exodus: Chapters 7 to 12.

God inflicted these sequential horrors after Pharaoh
refused to let Moses lead the Israelites out of Egypt
to freedom. It was only when God sent a plague in
which all the first-born, man and beast, died (with the
Israelites completely untouched) that Pharaoh allowed
the children of Israel, 600,000 of them, to leave.

Blood, Frogs, Lice, Pestilence, Flies,

Boils, Hail, Locusts, Darkness, First-born.

Beware Finding Licky Pesty Flies

Beware Handling Licky Dragon Flies

The Four Horsemen of the Apocalypse:

From the Book of Revelation 6:1-8

What Fool Picks Death?

War, Famine, Pestilence, Death.

The Seven Deadly Sins:

PALE GAS

Pride, Avarice, Lust, Envy, Gluttony, Anger, Sloth.

WASPLEG

Wrath, Avarice, Sloth, Pride, Lust, Envy, Gluttony.

Waspleg is the title of a good American book of mnemonics by Bart Benne published in 1988.

The Seven Deadly Sins are not referred to in a cohesive manner in the Bible, but have been a central feature of Catholicism for centuries, Pope Gregory the Great having codified them in the 6th-Century.

CHAPTER 13

Music

Guido of Arezzo (991 – 1033) is regarded as the father of modern musical notation: his solfeggio system became the forerunner of the Do-Re-Mi scale.

The Do-Re-Mi song from the Rodgers and Hammerstein musical and subsequent film The Sound of Music is a brilliant mnemonic for the eight notes in an octave.

Do, Re, Mi, Fa, So, La, Ti, Do

Doe, a deer, a female deer,

Ray, a drop of golden sun,

Me, a name I call myself,

Far, a long long way to run,

Sew, a needle pulling thread,

La, a note to follow so,

Tea, a drink with jam and bread

And that will bring us back to Doe.

Douglas Adams, the author of The Hitchhikers' Guide to the Galaxy, argued that Hammerstein put in the La line – A note to follow So – merely as a placeholder – he couldn't think of anything better or memorable, and so put that line in as a temporary measure meaning to go back to it sometime to improve it. He never did. Adams does have a point – all the other lines have a simple, wonderful beauty about them, except that one.

In an episode of the Simpsons, Homer crashes his car into the statue of a deer, whereupon he shouts 'D'oh', followed by Lisa, 'A deer' and Marge, 'A female deer'.

Notes:

On the lines of the treble clef:

EGBDF

Every Good Boy Deserves Favour

In the spaces of the treble clef:

FACE

On the lines of the bass clef:

GBDFA

Good Boys Deserve Fruit Always

Grizzly Bears Don't Fly Aeroplanes.

In the spaces of the bass clef:

All Cows Eat Grass

Progression:

Of sharps for sharp key signatures:

FCGDAEB

Father Charles Goes Down
And Ends Battle

One sharp, F, denotes the key of G. Two sharps, F and C, denote the key of D. Three sharps, F, C and G, denote the key of A, and so on

The designated key is one semi-tone above the last sharp on the key signature

Of flats for flat key signatures:

BEADGCF

Battle Ends And Down Goes
Charles's Father

Tuning a guitar:

EADGBE: (from the lowest string).

Every Able Dad Goes Bald Eventually

Elephants And Donkeys Grow Big Ears

Four sections of an orchestra:

Stringers Would Be Persecuted

Strings, Woodwind, Brass, Percussion

Choral Voices:

STAB

Soprano, Tenor, Alto, Bass.

Musical Modes:

I Don't Play Ludo Much After Lessons

Ionian, Dorian, Phrygian, Lydian, Mixolydian, Aeolian, Locrian.

The modes are scales dating from ancient Greece based on what became the white notes on the piano. The Ionian mode goes from C to C (the C major scale). The Dorian mode goes from E to E, and the Aeolian mode goes from A to A in the key of A minor.

CHAPTER 14

Things American

In fourteen hundred and ninety two,
Columbus sailed the ocean blue.
And found this land, land of the Free,
Beloved by you, beloved by me.

This is the start of a poem by Winifred Sackville
Stoner Jun (1902-1983) called The History of the U.S.

It goes on

Year seventeen hundred seventy six,
July the Fourth, this date please fix
Within your minds, my children dear,
for that was Independence Year.

The original 13 states:

My Nice New Car Needs Re-Painting.
Maybe Dark Violet? No, Shiny Gold

Massachusetts

New Hampshire

New York

Connecticut

New Jersey

Rhode Island

Pennsylvania

Maryland

Delaware

Virginia

North Carolina

South Carolina

Georgia

U.S. Presidents to 1849:

Washington's Army Journeyed Many Miles
And Just Battled Hard to Philadelphia.

Washington, George	1789-1797
Adams, John	1797 - 1801
Jefferson, Thomas	1801 - 1809
Madison, James	1809 - 1817
Monroe, James	1817 - 1825
Adams, John Quincy	1825 - 1829
Jackson, Andrew	1829 - 1837
Buren, Martin van	1837 - 1841
Harrison, William Henry - 1841	
Tyler, John	1841 - 1845
Polk, James Knox	1845 - 1849

U.S. Presidents 1849 – 1901:

To Find Pretty British Ladies,
Johnson Gave Him Good Advice:
Check Haagen-Dazs, Check Macy's

Taylor, Zachary	1849 - 1850
Fillmore, Millard	1850 - 1853
Pierce, Franklin	1853 -1857
Buchanan, James	1857 - 1861
Lincoln, Abraham	1861 - 1865
Johnson, Andrew	1865 - 1869
Grant, Ulysses Simpson	1869 - 1877
Hayes, Rutherford Birchard	1877 - 1881
Garfield, James Abram	1881
Arthur, Chester Alan	1881 - 1885
Cleveland, Grover	1885 - 1889
Harrison, Benjamin	1889 - 1893
Cleveland, Grover	1893 – 1897
McKinley, William	1897 - 1901

U.S. Presidents 1900 – 1945:

Roo Took What He Could Home, Right?

Roosevelt, Theodore	1901 - 1909
Taft, William Howard	1909 - 1913
Wilson, Woodrow	1913 - 1921
Harding, Warren Gamaliel	1921 - 1923
Coolidge, Calvin	1923 - 1929
Hoover, Herbert Clark	1929 - 1933
Roosevelt, Franklin Delano	1933 – 1945

U.S. Presidents 1945 onwards:

The Engineer Knew John Nixon's Ford
Could Really Be Clinton's Blue Oldsmobile

Truman, Harry S.	1945 - 1953
Eisenhower, Dwight	1953 - 1961
Kennedy, John Fitzgerald	1961 - 1963
Johnson, Lyndon Baines	1963 - 1969
Nixon, Richard Milhouse	1969 - 1974
Ford, Gerald	1974 -1977
Carter, James Earl	1977 - 1981
Reagan, Ronald	1981 - 1989
Bush, George Herbert Walker	1989 - 1993
Clinton, William Jefferson	1993 - 2001
Bush, George Walker	2001 - 2009
Obama, Barack	2009 -

Ten largest states:

Al texted Cally: MnMs Are
Never Coloured Orange. Why?

Alaska	Arizona
Texas	Nevada
California	Colorado
Montana	Oregon
New Mexico	Wyoming

Five smallest American states:

Rhodri's Delivered Connie's
New Jersey Near Hampton

Rhode Island, Delaware, Connecticut,

New Jersey, New Hampshire.

The Ivy League universities:

Your Data Base Contains Pretty Preppy Historic Colleges

Yale, Dartmouth, Brown, Cornell, Princeton, Penn (University of Pennsylvania), Harvard, Columbia.

A group of eight long-established, rich and prestigious colleges in the north east of the U.S. Ivy because of ivy-clad walls and League after intercollegiate football games were formalised into an official competition.

The Ivy League has been closely connected with the acronym WASP – White Anglo-Saxon Protestant - a powerful group who formed the social and political elite in the U.S. and were generally educated at an Ivy League college.

All American presidents have been male WASPs with the exception of President John Kennedy, who was a (very rich) Roman Catholic – a WASC if you want. And of course, Barack Obama, who rather broke the mould. But he did go to Harvard Law School.

CHAPTER 15

Acronyms & Abbreviations

Medical Acronyms:

About ten years ago there was a spate of newspaper stories about abbreviations, most of them in bad taste, that doctors were putting on patients' notes.

TATT

Tired All The Time

TEETH
Tried Everything Else, Try Homeopathy

WOT

Waste Of Time

LOBNH

Lights On But Nobody Home

CKBNDY

Completely Knackered, But Not Dead Yet

GOK

God Only Knows

(quite common, apparently)

FLK
Funny Looking Kid

GLM

Good Looking Mum

ARSD

Alcohol Related Sudden Death

PBAB

(An American one)

Pine Box at Bedside

TATSP

Thick as Two Short Planks

MAGGOT

Medically Able, Go Get Other Transportation

(on the notes of a patient who requested an ambulance home, but didn't need one).

GOMER

Get Out of My Emergency Room

(This is the name of the Press where this book was printed).

There were some regional variations as well:

NFN

Normal for Norfolk

Norfolk people had an undeserved reputation for being, well, eccentric.

NFA

Normal for Andover

This was from the hospital at Winchester, which obviously looked down its nose at its Hampshire neighbour.

And finally one that must have sent shivers down the spine of the medical staff.

KSI

Knows Somebody Important

Dr Phil Hammond, the TV doctor, was quoted as saying they had become something of an art form, but eventually they were banned. The UK Central Council for Nurse, Midwives and Health Visitors was forced to send out 640,000 letters warning medical staff not to use offensive jargon.

Acronyms:

YUPPIE

Young Urban Professional, popular in the 1980s but out of fashion now. It was ousted by

LOMBARD

Loads of Money But A Complete (fill in your own D-word)

Then the series became more family oriented:

DINKIES

Double Income, No Kids

SITCOM

Single Income, Two Children, Outrageous Mortgage

ORCHID

One Recent Child, Hideously In Debt

People from the computers systems and IT department have been known to leave notes on the back of office chairs. Family members have even been known to use it in reference to me.

PICNIC

Problem In Chair, Not In Computer

And a chauvinist warning that could come in useful in a darkened nightclub;

BOBFOC

Body off Baywatch, Face off Crimewatch

TWIRLY

Am I Too Early?

All people in England over 60 are eligible for free off-peak bus travel, which in most areas is from 9.30am to 11pm. Bus drivers have got very used to the pained question, at around 9.30 in the morning: Am I too early? (to qualify for the free travel concession?)

CHUK

An acronymic imperative from London stockbrokers Seymour Pierce to their clients on what to do with Choices UK shares.

SNAFU

Situation Normal, All Fouled Up (polite version)

MAMIL

Overheard at cash desk in cycle shop Halfords: 'Serve the Mamil at desk 2'.

Middle-Aged Man in Lycra

BIFFO

Big Ignorant Fellah From Offaly (polite version)

I first heard the BIFFO nickname 25 years ago. It was given to a big, blunt Fleet Street newspaper executive from Lancashire and stood for Big Ignorant Fellah From Oldham (also the polite version). The joke was that he thought it was meant as a term of endearment, Biffo being a cuddly anthropomorphic bear in the Beano comic dating back 50 years.

But it may be of Irish origin, because it is used as a fond and sometimes pejorative term for the natives of Offaly, a county in the south of Ireland. The Prime Minister of the Republic, Brian Cowen, is almost universally known as Biffo.

Not to be confused with BUFFALO

Big Ugly Fellah From Around Laois-Offaly (polite version again). Laois is an adjoining county.

SMIDSY:

An acronym used by London taxi-drivers in this fashion: I had another Smidsy today. It means that they were involved in a minor accident and that the other party said 'Sorry mate. I didn't see you.'

CRAFT:

A fitting entry for this book especially for those who experience senior moments.

Can't Remember A Flipping Thing (polite version)

Where should you sit on an aeroplane?

DAWN

Day Aisle, Window Night

Choose an aisle seat during the day so you can stretch your legs and move around a bit.

Choose a window seat in the night, so you sleep uninterrupted without people clambering all over you all night.

POSH:

Port Out, Starboard Home

There is no evidence that this was ever used on the luxury liners to and from Britain to the colonies in the Far East (the theory is that posh passengers would have been shaded from the sun in both directions), but as acronyms go, it is pretty neat. Rich passengers were said to have POSH stamped on their tickets, but there does not seem to be any truth in this. The liners were in service from the 1840s on, but it was 1918 before posh was first used to mean smart, exclusive and associated with the upper classes.

Here is a weird one. Paul Torday's follow-up book to his bestselling Salmon Fishing In Yemen was The Irresistible Inheritance Of Wilberforce.

His hero was so deluded and delusioned that he could only remember what happened to his wife by the mnemonic:

TNMWWTTW

The Night My Wife Went Through The Windscreen

Well I said it was weird.

MOM-G

Although not a mnemonic, it's a very useful secret acronym.

It's Welsh:

Mas O 'Ma – Gloi.

Get Out Of Here – Quick!

Checklists:

For aircraft:

CIGAR

Controls, Instruments, Gas, Altitude indicator, Radio

For landing:

GUMPS

Gas, Undercarriage, Mixture, Pilot strapped in, Speed

BUMFH

Australian variation of GUMPS

Brakes, Undercarriage, Mixture, Fuel, Hatches and Harnesses

Starting a long car journey:

PETROL

Petrol, Electrolyte (battery), Tyres, Radiator, Oil, Lights

Survival expert Ray Mears's mnemonic for checking his vehicle was OK before setting out on a journey, which in his case was generally a bit more than popping out to the local shop.

And for motorbikes

BOLTS

Brakes, Oil, Lights, Tyres, Steering and Suspension

For small children:

Hideous Fools, Morons, Keep Silent!

This is the Nanny's Mnemonic – I'm glad we never had nannies like that. But it's not as bad as it sounds. It's the checklist for ensuring their charges are presentable.

Hair brushed?

Face washed?

Middle neat?

Knees clean?

Shoes brushed and tied?

Backronyms:

A backronym is a word used as a acronym although it wasn't originally intended as one.

The Apgar Test earlier in the book (P. 124) was a backronym, because a doctor named Apgar devised a test for the health of new-born babies, and the five letters in her surname were used – ten years later – to create an acronym. If the doctor had been called Smith, we wouldn't have an acronym for the test

The most famous backronym is SOS – Save Our Souls or Save Our Ship. It comes from the Morse Code (See P.164), which was made up of dots and dashes. The code for S was dot dot dot and for O dash dash dash. So dot dot dot dash dash dash dot dot dot became the Morse code distress signal.

The SOS distress signal was first adopted by Germany in 1905 and became the international standard in 1908. The Germans chose the code for its simplicity; it had nothing to do with the letters the code represented. It was only later that an English backronym was attached to the code.

Another backronym which was current some time ago was for Ford cars: First on Race Day if you liked them, Found on Road, Dead, if you didn't.

CHAPTER 16

The Life of Pi

Pi deserves its own little section for the sheer volume of mnemonics.

It is the 16th letter of the Greek alphabet and owes its fame to the fact that it is the symbol of the ratio of the circumference of a circle to its diameter – an infinite number 22 over 7. To four decimal places it is 3.1415

Area of a circle:

Apple Pies Are Square

Area = πr^2

Circumference of a circle:

Cherry Pie Delicious

Circumference = πd

The following mnemonics are all based on counting the number of letters in each word of a sentence, or verse.

To six decimal places:

How I wish I could calculate pi

3.141592

To seven places:

May I have a large container of coffee

3.1415926

Pi to 14 places:

How I want a drink, alcoholic of course,

After the heavy chapters

Involving quantum mechanics.

3.14159265358979

To 30 decimal places:

(From the Mensa Journal).

Sir, I send a rhyme excelling

In sacred truth and rigid spelling;

Numerical sprites elucidate

All my own striving can't relate

If nature gain

Not you complain

Tho' Dr Johnson fulminate

3.141592653589793238462643383279

For the reciprocal of pi:

Can I remember the reciprocal?

0.318310

Pi certainly brings out something in the scientific world: there are hundreds of websites devoted to the little Greek letter. And a number of them give pi to one million decimal places. In September 2010, it was reported that a Japanese systems engineer had calculated the value of pi to five trilllion (5,000,000,000,000) decimal places, breaking the previous record of 2.7 trillion. His computer took 90 days to reach the figure but it did not impress his wife - she pointed out that the project had enormously increased their electricity bill.

In America quite a number of people celebrate Pi Day on March 14 (3.14) which also happens to be Albert Einstein's birthday. There is also another unofficial holiday called Pi Approximation Day that is on July 22 (22/7). The celebrations generally involve eating pies.

CHAPTER 17

The Miscellany Box

The G8 countries:

The Group of Eight is made up of the governments of Canada, France, Germany, Italy, Japan, Russia, the United Kingdom and the U.S. The European Union is also represented at meetings. These eight countries contain about 14 per cent of the world's population yet control more than 65 per cent of the world's economic output.

GUS CUK FRIJ

Germany	France
United States	Russia
Canada	Italy
United Kingdom	Japan

The members of OPEC

The members of the Organisation of Petroleum Exporting Countries control about two thirds of the world's oil reserves.

EQUI- VALANSKI

Ecuador	Libya
Qatar	Angola
United Arab Emirates	Nigeria
Iraq	Saudi Arabia
Venezuela	Kuwait
Algeria	Iran

This Russian-sounding mnemonic is slightly ironic, because Russia, one of the world's biggest oil producers, is not a member.

Dewey Decimal
Library Classification:

The system is made up of ten main categories, each
divided into ten sub-categories, each of which is further
divided into ten sub-divisions. The ten main categories
are:

General Phil Reckoned Social Language
Should Treat Art Like History

000 - General

100 - Philosophy

200 - Religion

300 - Social Sciences

400 - Languages

500 - Science

600 - Technology

700 - The Arts

800 - Literature

900 - History

The Most Distinguished Order of St Michael and St George:

Founded in 1818 by George, Prince Regent, who later became George IV. Originally for the inhabitants of the Ionian Islands and Malta, later for any official in colonial affairs and the foreign and diplomatic service.

There are three classes of the order:

3　Companion of the Order of
St Michael and St George:

CMG: Call Me God

2　Knight/Dame Commander of the Order
of St Michael and St George:

KCMG: Kindly Call Me God

1　Knight/Dame Grand Cross
of the Order of St Michael and St George

GCMG : God Calls Me God

Lord Baden-Powell, who was awarded the GCMG in 1927, always described recipients of the CMG as Colonial Made Gentlemen.

Titles:

Did Marky Ever Visit Barmouth Beach?

Duke, Marquis, Earl, Viscount, Baron, Baronet.

Only sons of dukes and marquises, and daughters of dukes, marquises and earls can use their Christian names in their titles. Thus Lady Diana Spencer was a lady in her own right, being the daughter of an Earl.

Viscounts and barons use the title Lord and their wives Lady, but never with their Christian name. The life peer Lord Owen is the politician David Owen and, not being the son of a duke or marquis, he is never Lord David Owen (as he was on the BBC news recently). His wife, Debbie, is Lady Owen or Debbie Owen.

For some reason television is the worst culprit in this matter – hardly a day goes by in these pre-Olympic times without a reference to Sebastian Coe as Lord Sebastian Coe. Lord Coe has had a varied career, being a world-record and Olympic gold medal-winning middle distance runner, and then a Conservative MP, and now the head of the successful bid to hold the Olympic Games in London in 2012. But what he never was was the son of a duke or marquis and I am sure that he would not want people to think he was.

Sir Richard Branson can be known as Sir Richard or Richard Branson. His wife is Lady Branson or Joan, but never Lady Joan Branson. If life peers keep more than one name, they must hyphenate it, which means in

House of Lords protocol it becomes one word. When Andrew Lloyd Webber is lording it, he is called Lord Lloyd-Webber.

The Premier Cru wines of Bordeaux:

Teletubby jabbed by a pencil (Lala, MMR, HB).

Lala: Chateau Latour (Pauillac)
        Chateau Lafite Rothschild (Pauillac)
MMR: Chateau Margaux (Margaux)
        Chateau Mouton-Rothschild (Pauillac)
HB: Chateau Haut-Brion (Graves)

In 1855 by order of Napoleon III, the wines of the Medoc were classified into five divisions, but of the thousands of wines submitted, only 60 were thought worthy of classification and only four wines were granted premier grand cru status (one of which, Haut-Brion, was not from the Medoc, but from Graves). The classification has remained unchanged since, save that Mouton-Rothschild was admitted to the first rank in 1973.

These are the best wines in the world, but they are fantastically expensive: as I write, should you be interested, Berry Brothers have a bottle of 1982 Chateau Lafite Rothschild available for £5,250 (inc VAT). You'd better hurry – there are only three bottles left.

Ant and Dec:

Some people who may think this is important find it difficult to tell the ubiquitous television presenters apart as they are always together. The Bill Nighy character in Love Actually, who didn't know which was which, (or perhaps he elided them into one person), addresses them: AntorDec.

Ant (Anthony David McPartlin) is always on the left on the TV

Dec (Declan Joseph Oliver Donnelly) is on the right.

This follows the 180 degree rule, which is a basic film editing principle that two people in the same scene should always have the same left/right relationship to each other. They seem to have taken this rule to the nth degree, as in almost all of their TV appearances, Ant is on the left and Dec on the right.

A is before D in the alphabet, so start from left with A.

Also: Ant = Anterior, to the fore, the one with the big fore-head.

Dec = Decrease, getting smaller, the smaller one.

The Harry Potter Books:

This is very useful in remembering the names and the order of JK Rowling's series of seven world best-selling books. It comes in handy remembering the films, too.

Please Can Pupils

in Gryffindor

Open Harry's Door?

1 HP and the Philosopher's Stone

2 HP and the Chamber of Secrets

3 HP and the Prisoner of Azkaban

4 HP and the Goblet of Fire

5 HP and the Order of the Phoenix

6 HP and the Half-blood Prince

7 HP and the Deathly Hallows

It looks as if the seventh book is going to be filmed in two parts, but we will cross that bridge when we get to it.

Creature Collections

Some of this entry will surely come in useful one day. It is part of a list of 75 compiled by a late colleague Nigel Thomas as an addition to the style- book at The Mail on Sunday. Many date back to the 15th century.

A shrewdness of Apes

A sounder of Boars

A tok of Capercailzies

A cluster of Cats

A covert of Coots

A murder of Crows

A charm of Finches

A skulk of Foxes

An army of Frogs

A trip of Goats

A cast of Hawks

An array of Hedgehogs

A siege of Herons

A glean of Herrings

A drift of Hogs

A smack of Jellyfish

A kindle of Kittens

An exaltation of Larks

A tiding of Magpies

A labour of Moles

A barren of Mules

A watch of Nightingales

A muster of Peacocks

A wickedness of Ravens

A crash of Rhinoceroses

A parliament of Rooks

A murmuration of Starlings

A bevy of Swans

A knot of Toads

A pitying of Turtledoves

A fall of Woodcocks

The genre lends itself to some modern-day homo sapiens examples: A bevy of Alcoholics, an attitude of Teenagers and a brace of Orthodontists.

Letter	Morse	Mnemonic		Letter	Morse	Mnemonic
A	*di-dah*	aLONE	N	*dah dit*	NAUGHty
B	*dah-di-di-dit*	BEAUtifully	O	*dah-dah-dah*	OUR OLD OAK
C	*dah-di-dah-dit*	COME a CROPper	P	*di-dah-dah-dit*	PoLITE PERson
D	*dah-di-dit*	DAINtily	Q	*dah-dah-di-dah*	QUITE QUEER and QUAINT
E	*dit*	Egg	R	*di-dah-dit*	ReWARDing
F	*di-di-dah-dit*	For a FORTnight	S	*di-di-dit*	Sh sh sh
G	*dah-dah-dit*	GOOD GRACious	T	*dah*	Tea
H	*di-di-di-dit*	Ha ha ha ha	U	*di-di-dah*	underNEATH
I	*di-dit*	Is it?	V	*di-di-di-dah*	Very verBOSE
J	*di-dah-dah-dah*	JaPAN'S JAM JARS	W	*di-dah-dah*	WithOUT WASTE
K	*dah-di-dah*	KISS me KATE	X	*di-dah-dah-dit*	ExTRA EXpense
L	*di-dah-di-dit*	LiNOleum	Y	*dah-dah-di-dah*	YELLOW yacht's YARN
M	*dah-dah*	MY MATE	Z	*dah-dah-di-dit*	ZEB-ZEB ra-ra

The Morse Code:

A binary code for transmitting messages, devised by US inventor Samuel Morse in 1837. Each letter has its own unique combination of dots (short) and dashes (long). See Backronyms p.148.

MORSE – a visual mnemonic

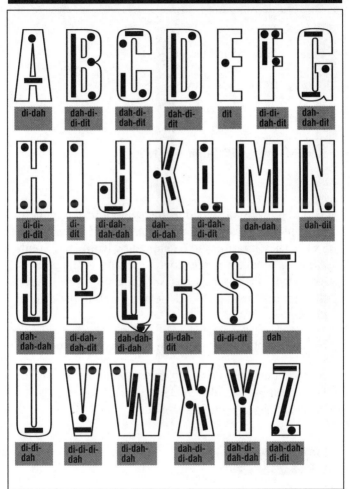

A di-dah	**B** dah-di-di-dit	**C** dah-di-dah-dit
D dah-di-dit	**E** dit	**F** di-di-dah-dit
G dah-dah-dit		

H di-di-di-dit	**I** di-dit	**J** di-dah-dah-dah
K dah-di-dah	**L** di-dah-di-dit	**M** dah-dah
N dah-dit		

O dah-dah-dah	**P** di-dah-dah-dit	**Q** dah-dah-di-dah
R di-dah-dit	**S** di-di-dit	**T** dah

U di-di-dah	**V** di-di-di-dah	**W** di-dah-dah
X dah-di-di-dah	**Y** dah-di-dah-dah	**Z** dah-dah-di-dit

Colours of the Olympic Rings:

Blue, Yellow, Black, Green, Red

in order from left to right

BY BGR

Records are set BY jumping BiGgeR

The rings were designed as the symbol of the modern Olympic Games by Baron Pierre de Coubertin in 1912. They represent five continents: North and South America count as one continent, and Antarctica is excluded. Bit harsh on the Antarcticans – you'd have thought they would have done quite well in the Winter Olympics.

No continent is represented by any specific colour.

A trick question in a pub quiz could be: What are Olympic gold medals made of?
Answer: Silver, well 92.5 per cent.

First Aid:

ABC – traditional method of checking what to do to treat a casualty.

Airways, Breathing, Circulation

BBB — after an accident, what to check in what order.

Breath Before Blood,

Blood Before Bones

When the face is red, raise the head;

When the face is pale, raise the tail.

The Spleen

You don't often get spleen and beautiful in the same sentence. So how about this beautiful, perfect mnemonic for the spleen?

1, 3, 5, 7, 9, 11

One inch by three inches by five inches in size. Seven ounces in weight. Lies between the ninth and eleventh ribs.

Body types:

ENDomorphs have big ENDs

Mesomorphs are Muscular

EcTomorphs are Thin

The order of suits in Bridge:

Sue Hates Dealing Cards

Spades, Hearts, Diamonds, Clubs

Bulls and Bears in the City:

BUlls are BUyers.

They are bullish, they are optimists. Prices are going to go up.

BUy. BUy. BUy.

BEars are sEllers.

They are realists. Prices are going to go down.

sEll. sEll. sEll.

Units of Alcohol

The amount of alcohol in drinks is measured in units, one unit in the UK being 10 ml (8gms) of pure alcohol. People seem to have trouble working out how much alcohol is in a particular drink. It is simple to calculate the amount of units in any drink: think of that nice museum in South Kensington:

V&A = U

Multiply together the Volume of the drink in litres and the Alcohol by volume of the drink.

So for example, an average glass, 150ml (0.150l), of white wine, typically 12% ABV, is 0.150 x 12 = 1.8 units.

A 440ml can of lager, typically 5% ABV, will be 2.2 units, and a pint of beer (568ml, say 3.5%) is 1.98 units.

The Government-recommended safe daily limit for men is 3 to 4 units a day, and 2 to 3 units a day for women. But not for driving.

Firewood:

A big old ash tree blew down in the wind in our garden recently, and a friend who was staying with us, said it was the best wood to burn bar none. And he sent me a poem which made the same point:

Beech wood fires burn bright and clear

If the logs are kept a year;

Store your beech for Christmastide

With new-cut holly laid beside;

Chestnut's only good, they say,

If for years 'tis stored away;

Birch and fir wood burn too fast

Blaze too bright and do not last;

Flames from larch will shoot up high,

Dangerously the sparks will fly;

But ash wood green and ash wood brown

Are fit for a Queen with a golden crown.

Oaken logs, if dry and old,

Keep away the winter's cold;

Poplar gives a bitter smoke,

Fills your eyes and makes you choke;

Elmwood burns like churchyard mould.

E'en the very flames are cold;

Hawthorn bakes the sweetest bread –

So it is in Ireland said;

Apple wood will scent the room,

Pear wood smells like flowers in bloom;

But ash wood wet and ash wood dry

A King may warm his slippers by.

So you can burn ash wood wet or dry, seasoned or not.
It really is the best wood to burn.

Basic DIY:

Which way to screw a screw or open a jar.

Righty tighty, leftie loosie

Flower arranging - 1

You've been waiting for this one all your life, especially if you have a close friend called Colin.

Colin Tells Such Fat Lies:

This is for the elements of design in flower arranging

Colour, Texture, Space, Form, Line

Flower arranging - 2

Putting Cut flowers in water:

The Harder the stem, the Hotter the water.

Deciduous and coniferous trees:

Deciduous trees Drop their leaves in autumn.

The others don't.

Deciduous can also describe ants that shed their wings after copulation.

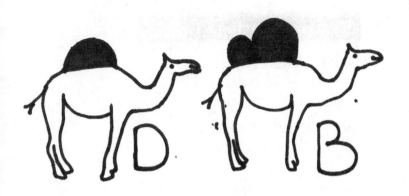

Camels:

Bactrian camel – two humps – capital B on its side

Dromedary – one hump – capital D on its side

Elephants:

As Africa is much bigger than India, so African elephants are much bigger than Indian elephants. The ears of both are shaped like their respective continents.

The novels of Jane Austen:

JanE AustEn

His Lady PPS's NAME - PERson

The History of England

Lady Susan

Pride and Prejudice

Sense and Sensibility

Northanger Abbey

Mansfield Park

Emma

Persuasion

Sanditon

Chess

White is right

The colour of the square of each player's right hand corner.

Bee and wasp stings:

Ammonia for a Bee sting - AB

Vinegar for a Wasp sting - VW

This is a long-standing mnemonic but there appears to be no evidence to show that vinegar is effective for wasp stings (although it seems to work with jellyfish stings).

The NHS Direct advice for a wasp sting is: wash the area, apply an ice pack, raise affected part, take antihistamine if necessary.

All right– so does the famous Rugby Union Club London Wasps have a B team? They probably have, and they could still play in the same colours – yellow and black.

Snooker:

You Go Brown By Potting Black

The sequence of the six colours after all the red balls have been potted

Yellow, Green, Brown, Blue, Pink, Black.

French:

A useful way to remember the main verbs which are compounded with etre in the perfect tense is

MMT Draper's Van

Monter, Mourir, Tomber. Descendre, Rester, Arriver, Partir, Entrer, Retourner, Sortir. Venir, Aller, Naitre.

Latin:

You may be asked at some stage the meaning of the beautiful Latin phrase, attributed to Thomas á Kempis (1418)

Sic transit gloria mundi

It does not mean Gloria was sick in the van on Monday.

The phrase is properly translated:

Thus passes the glory of the world

(Worldly things do not last for ever).

CHAPTER 18

Postscript

I once worked on a newspaper in the North of England and in the taperoom were two chaps whose names I always mixed up. It was embarrassing because I had dealings with them every day.

One was called Terry, who was always smartly dressed with a jacket and tie, and always, I remember, polished shoes. He became the Toff.

The other was called John. He was always casually dressed, with open-neck shirt and trainers – and he looked a bit dopey. He became the Jerk.

They couldn't have looked much more different if they had tried, but I'm sorry, the only way I could remember their names was to think of Toff – Terry and Jerk – John. Sorry, Terry and John.

We moved house once and had to change the telephone number. I got a number of options from the girl at the telephone exchange, one of which was – well, the way she said it – XX1 066. She offered me others, but then something clicked and I said I'll have XX 1066.

The year 1066 – the Battle of Hastings – is one of the most famous and memorable dates in British history. Oh, that's a good number she said, but because she was reading the numbers in groups of three, she hadn't seen it. Nor had other people who had wanted a new number, because it was still available.

It's not much, but it is an example of how you can sort and rearrange everyday data – for example it's very useful in remembering PINs – to make life a little easier.

On a completely prosaic note to end, it's easy enough and I find, very useful, to make up little mnemonics in your everyday life. Say I have four things to do - in no particular order– take a Pill, write to the Bank, email a friend (Robert), and ring School, I will make up something like this:

PSBR: This used to be, and maybe it still is, the Public Sector Borrowing Requirement – take a Pill, ring School, write to the Bank, email Robert.

GBP: Great Britain Pounds: Don't forget to take a Pill, (a pattern is emerging here), phone the Garage and buy some Bread.

The aim of this book has been to be a useful, informative, practical and I hope enjoyable and entertaining way of recalling and remembering bits and pieces of data. If you are really serious about increasing the power of your memory, there are a number of memory systems of varying complexity that will eventually allow you to create a prodigious memory. Tony Buzan, the British memory expert, identifies five different peg systems and has produced many successul books on these systems.

Happy memorising.

Bibliography

A Dictionary of Mnemonics, 1972

Benne, B: Waspleg and other Mnemonics, 1988

Buchan, J: As Easy as Pi, 2009

Cook, V: Accomodating Brocolli in the Cemetary, 2004

Dummett, M: Grammar and Style, 1993

Evans, RL: Every Good Boy Deserves Fudge, 2007

Ferraro, S: Remembrance of Things Fast, 1990

Foley, E and Coates, B: Homework for Grown-ups, 2008

Fowler, HW and FG: The King's English, reprinted 1993

Gordon, K: The Transitive Vampire, 1984

Gowers, Sir E: The Complete Plain Words, 1970

Grey, R: Memoria Technica, c 1760 reprint 1827

Heffer, S: Strictly English, 2010

Hughes, T: By Heart, 100 Poems to Remember, 1997

I wish I knew that, 2010

Lamb, BC: The Queen's English, 2010

Parkinson, J: i before e (except after c), 2007

Parkinson, J: Remember, remember the Fifth of November, 2008

Parkinson, J: Spilling the Beans on the Cat's Pyjamas, 2009

Partridge, E: Usage and Abusage – A guide to good English,1999

Phythian, BA: Foreign Expressions, 1982

Sampson, A (ed): I wandered Lonely as a Cloud, 2009

Sellers, L: The Simple Subs Book, 1968

Spence, JD: The Memory Palace of Matteo Ricci, 1984

Spiegel, F: Sick Notes, 1996

Taggart, C: An Apple a Day, 2009

Taggart, C: Guide to the Queen's English, 2010

Taggart, C: I Used to Know That, 2008

The Oxford Dictionary for Writers and Editors, 1981

Thirty Days has September, 2008

Thomson, AJ and Martinet, AV: Practical English Grammar, 1990

Toseland, M; A Steroid Hit the Earth, 2008

Truss, L: Eats, Shoots & Leaves, 2003

Waterhouse, K: Waterhouse on Newspaper Style, 1989

NOTES